The Surfer's Guide To Marketing

How to Avoid Wiping Out
In the Marketing Space

By

Randy Rovegno

Dedicated to my family.

Without my soul mate Heather and my favorite groms Dillan and Sawyer, I would have wiped out long ago.

"It is better to have surfed and wiped out than to have never surfed at all."
- Willis Brothers

CONTENTS

FOREWORD

I appreciate when someone can put a new spin on traditional views. That is how I have approached my life and experienced great rewards as a result.

The other thing that is imperative to remember is to trust yourself even when it can be scary pursuing uncharted waters. Randy uses surfing as a great teacher and provides interesting analogies to communicate his marketing philosophies in his book.

- Laird Hamilton

"Surfing is a special kind of madness, a feeling for the sea, a combination of love, knowledge, respect, fear - instinctive perception gained through repeated contact."

- Tom Curren

INTRODUCTION (SURF'S UP)

I have been a marketing executive for two decades and an avid surfer for about half of that time. And as far as surfing goes, I'm a much better marketer. (I've never ended up in the ER with a dozen stitches in my rear end from any of the marketing campaigns I've created). As a 6'4" clumsy 40-something, I have been referred to as "*The Yeti from the Jetty*" who paddles out with a board so big that it should have a galley downstairs. But, like my career, I approach every day, every wave, and every ride as an opportunity to improve on what I have done in the past, put forth my best effort, and most of all enjoy what I am doing. If you don't enjoy the ride, get out of the water.

You don't need to be a knowledgeable surfing expert to read this book. In fact, I simply found that there were many similarities between my favorite hobby and my chosen profession and that I could hopefully utilize the analogies to express various business, marketing, and communication principles and tactics in a unique perspective.

This approach works well when I lecture to college students at USC, Pepperdine, Chico State, and other institutions and I have found that presenting unique and proven marketing practices in the form of more tangible (and just plain interesting) examples makes for a very positive experience. Most of the basic fundamentals and marketing approaches are outlined ad nauseam in the various text books and lessons that the college curriculum requires and since I've never read a book I didn't color in, I have simply sculpted a combination of my own successful experiences with proven theories and principles. Adding case studies featuring famous celebrities, Super Bowl events, and the hottest television shows as real-world examples of applying the book's tactics provides a more colorful and digestible lesson. So in essence, by talking surf, we can illustrate some of my favorite and proven marketing strategies.

The goal in creating *The Surfer's Guide To Marketing* was three-fold;

1) **Communicate** various marketing tactics, secrets, and approaches that we have activated in the field and have been real-world battle tested. While some books use a lot of pages to discuss marketing *theory*, I have always utilized real-world examples and case studies that provide proven results instead of possibilities. Throughout *The Surfer's Guide To Marketing* you will find CASE STUDIES that demonstrate the topics at hand with actual marketing campaigns or tactics as well as SURF LESSONS that provide more of a tutorial and application element to have the reader take an active role in the discussion. These active lessons will challenge the reader to participate rather than just recite the tactics and ensure that this book provides tangible value.

While due to legal reasons, I may not be able to give you the names of all the projects, the clients, or other specific (re: incriminating) details, rest assured just as the Pacific Ocean is cold as hell on a January morning, they are all real, proven examples. It's very important for me to have the reader realize that the various concepts, tactics, examples, cases, and lessons are actual proven experiences of how to succeed without wiping out!

2) **Motivate** the inner-marketing genius in all of us. By showing a variety of both complex and simple solutions to some of the most common obstacles found in the competitive business landscape, we can demonstrate that, like every surfer that has ever paddled out, you will get knocked down a few times and it's ultimately how you ride the next wave that counts. Some of the cases and interviews are amazing and will showcase that both expert marketers and rookie entrepreneurs can succeed when things seem difficult. So why not use the hundreds of gallons of salt water I've swallowed learning how to surf to your advantage and jump in after I've tested the waters!

3) **Entertain** you with some true tales of grandeur from the world of marketing and surfing along with my own humorous tales ranging from longboards to board meetings. After all, it's ok to smile, have some fun and absorb the message without being bored to tears.

Having been fortunate enough to work on some amazing campaigns with incredible brands like *Disney, ESPN, Upper Deck, NFL, Chevy, ABC*, and with a resume of creating award-winning efforts with such talent as Drew Brees, Michael Jordan, George Lopez, Ray Romano, and hundreds more, I have been blessed with the passion, creativity, and ability to bring unique concepts to life. And while I have come up against both the expected as well as the unforeseen obstacles that every marketer inevitably endures throughout his or her career, I have always found that certain tactics can help overcome adversity and serve as a proven template for success. Just as a surfer uses different boards for different conditions or different surf spots, I will hopefully provide some successful marketing strategies that can be used when you paddle out into the ocean of marketing.

We will explore a variety of different approaches and some of the challenges we have faced along the way. Some of the various efforts may be similar to your situation and perhaps *The Surfer's Guide To Marketing* can help you develop strategic solutions based on a variety of different approaches or actual samples found in the book. And just as every surf break has its own set of challenges, your particular marketing needs or experience may differ from some of the discussion points in the book which is also a great opportunity to use this as a motivational resource to attack your own unique circumstances.

Attitude, having the proper perspective, is one of the most important tools in any marketer's arsenal and just like a big wave surfer who drops in on a 20-foot face, you need the proper mind set and confidence to pull it off. Just as there is no perfect board for all waves, there is no blanket approach for every group's marketing needs and as they say, invention is 1% inspiration and 99% perspiration. So along with samples of how brands succeeded in various situations and environments, my goal is to get your marketing mind churning, get your creative juices flowing, and put you in a positive, optimistic mindset so that you have the ability to catch the big wave and still live to tell about it.

Surf's up!

"I took off on a wave, went down the side, popped out the other end, and went, s***, I'm still alive!"
- Greg Noll

CHAPTER 1

PUFFER FISH

Size matters. In surfing, the very sport is measured on metrics; the height of a wave, the length of a board, the duration of a ride. You don't need to be a seasoned marketer to understand that the larger the campaign, the agency, the budget, etc. the greater the volume, revenue, or importance. This section is going to focus on the smaller marketer's attitude and resourcefulness.

In the surfing world, a two-foot ankle-slapper doesn't garner much interest beyond the surfers who enjoy a fun ride but as the size builds, so does the amount of interest (See the BIG WAVES chapter). But ask any seasoned surfer and they will say that the small waves can be as rewarding as the large monsters and it's all in how you view it, experience it, and most of all surf it.

This chapter is an exploration of the 80/20 rule where the majority of marketing groups and professionals (the 80% of the business world) does not have huge budgets yet must compete with the large blue-chip organizations that seldom use "competition is too large" as a barrier to entry. While the budgets of 2007 have evaporated and even the former Big Kahunas of the marketing world have experienced more shrinkage than a cold morning in the Pacific, they still have the resources to create and activate significant efforts. Some claim lack of funds or other resources despite great brands and in fact, I have a major television network client who often asks if I can do work for free (I'm no CPA but I do wonder how my small agency, LONGBOARD Marketing, can have a larger marketing budget than one of the most powerful broadcast companies in the world?). But exceptions aside, this chapter is focused on cultivating unique opportunities for the "Mom and Pop" retailers, the small restaurants, boutique agency, or the start up clothing line to compete in the established world.

While you may have a great idea, innovative product, or solid strategy, it doesn't always ensure success. Every day I paddle out and watch some skinny 13-year-old cut up and down a face effortlessly, yet when I attempt to do a similar move, it looks nothing like that. In fact, while I understand the fundamentals and pop up on my board the exact same way a pro does, I often find myself drinking salt water at the bottom of the ocean in a futile waste of time, energy, and effort.

It's this common wipeout, or the fear of it, that swallows up small to mid-sized marketing efforts. They don't have the experience, strength, tools, or just plain good fortune to drop in and ride a successful wave across the business landscape. And often times they don't have the right mindset, confidence or even insight into little adjustments that could have them leading to a successful ride and that lack of confidence can cause paralysis by analysis. Along with being small or inexperienced, the worse result is that others perceive their lack of courage as an inability to fulfill their customer's needs. There is nothing worse than losing out on distribution, a new client, or revenue because they think you can't handle their business, create enough product, or are just too small.

Perhaps with a slight weight shift, different take off

point, or a different surfboard they could succeed in the exact same environment. It's a combination of having the confidence to paddle out and the appearance of looking big enough to compete and succeed with your competition. Smaller brands simply need to appear more seasoned, have resources, or just appear *bigger.*

Herein lies the **Puffer Fish**. I will touch on ways to become a **Puffer Fish** shortly, but first, let's talk about the attitude necessary to succeed as a small player. While I don't advocate making foolish or impulsive marketing decisions, there are times where we cannot decisively ensure that our plan will work. We analyze the opportunity, the environment, the competition, etc. and then make that leap of faith. Just like coming over the lip of a large wave and seeing a harrowing combination of salt water and your life flash before your eyes, it takes guts and commitment to pull the trigger.

Eddie Aikiu was a legendary surfer from Hawaii. In 1978, Aikiu was a member of the crew that ran into trouble in the Pacific when their boat began to sink. In need of help, Eddie took his surfboard and set off in an attempt to paddle to Lanai to get help. Unfortunately, he was never seen again. But his attitude, confidence, and flat out heroism spawned the mantra *"Eddie Would Go"*. I'm not saying that marketers should risk life and limb but you must also have the wholehearted belief that you can and will succeed based on your abilities.

One of the biggest flaws in business is self-doubt. Not providing the support, resources, or fortitude necessary to truly support a campaign, initiative, or new idea. While some people like your boss or CEO may sign off on the budget or give the green light, are they truly putting their wholehearted confidence behind the effort? Show me a surfer who drops in at Pipeline with 50% effort on a big day and I will show you a surfer who is going to wipe out 100% of the time.

The attitude of the **Puffer Fish** is exactly that; if you think you are big, you can be big. If you think you have the strategy, creativity, hustle, common sense, or just better offerings than the next guy, you need to exude confidence in that belief. While the saying *"fake it 'till you make it"* comes to mind, I would suggest that we refer to being a smaller fish as our ability to hunt like a great white while trapped in the body of a minnow. (And hope we never get trapped inside the body of great white!) It's not the size of the fish in the fight, but the size of the fight in the fish. I'd put those mean little Bettas that live in *Dixie cup*-sized containers at the pet store up against fish ten times their size. If you believe you are big, and have the ability to perform well beyond your current capabilities, then you are indeed a prime candidate to act like a **Puffer Fish**.

The **Puffer Fish** strategy is simple; gather whatever resources and skills you do have access to and leverage them incrementally beyond their individual worth. The sum of the parts is greater than the whole.

I liken the **Puffer Fish** approach to those outdoor adventure television shows where the explorer takes inventory of the tools and resources they have available. They may not have a tent, boat, or lighter but in a MacGyver-esque moment, they can use the stick of gum and shoelace they have to escape the Amazon jungle. **Puffer Fish** marketing has the same mentality; it's not what we need, but rather what we have. Perhaps you have access to inexpensive digital buys or in-house creative that would cost significantly more if you outsourced it. If you are a small product, you may be able to provide samples or BOGO deals in lieu of paying straight cash for slotting fees. Whatever you have available to leverage your brands or your offer, then that will be the "air" in your **Puffer Fish** approach.

In today's global instant-communication culture, you don't need to be a huge company with your own warehouse, factory, army of employees, etc. Virtual offices allow smaller sized marketers to seamlessly perform grandiose efforts formerly reserved for those with millions of dollars in assets. A freelance creative team can send files electronically to sub-contracted printers who handle fulfillment and manage your shipping, payroll, etc. all from the laptop in your garage.

As long as you have enough support to actually fulfill the promise or agreement you have presented, then you can appear larger than you actually are. It may be more effort than traditional competitors are putting forth but your creativity, fortitude, and talent can exponentially exceed expectations if you believe you can and you show a little swagger.

LONGBOARD Marketing, my Sports & Entertainment Marketing agency, often walks into pitch meetings in direct competition with *BBDO, Wieden & Kennedy, GMR*, etc. With today's graphics, software, and our small team's unsurpassed creative, we compete with "big boys" simply by showing presentations that are as good (or frankly better) than any of the competition. We promote our strengths incrementally to disguise our size and focus on the work, the brands in our portfolio, and our strength… creativity.

While every meeting inevitably has questions about our agency's size, we are quickly able to turn the focus back on our abilities, not the amount of bodies it takes to execute. We carry ourselves like a larger agency and focus on our **Puffer Fish** strengths which happen to include the use of **Starfish**, or famous talent (see the CASE STUDY at the end of this chapter and significantly more celebrity marketing in the STARFISH chapter). Our capabilities presentation features examples of work we've done with Evander Holyfield,

Ray Romano, Ronnie Lott, Nick Lachey, etc. for the sole purpose of instilling in potential clients a belief that "LONGBOARD Marketing *must* be a major agency if they do promotions with Marcus Allen, Tony Romo, and Bruce Jenner". It simply leverages our strength as a key selling point and allows us to discuss the same level of talent that *CAA* or *IMG* utilizes. And if we are a boutique group that is perceived as being equal to huge agencies, then we have already won!

To the average fan, every professional surfer competing in an ASP event looks amazing! So how does Kelly Slater win 11 World Championships? What sets him apart? Does he have that extra skill or God-given talent? Or, if all things are equal, does the Kelly Slater *name* hold some subconscious advantage in the minds of judges? NBA officials give superstars more calls than rookies and it's just a common practice accepted in the league. The name on the back of the jersey can be a very persuasive argument. Think of the superstars as the established brands in the market and the smaller marketers as a rookie sixth-man on the league's worst team. You simply need to work twice as hard and simply create the impression that you are equal to LeBron James. If the gap is significant between the All-Stars and the free agents, then the name, exposure and reputation can only serve to expand the parity and make the perception even greater than the actuality.

A small percentage of surfboard manufacturers dominate the category but while an expert surfer can feel the difference between the boards' rails or shape, it's the *Quiksilver* logo or the *Robert August* name that drives the sale. Brand recognition is a key to success as any marketer will tell you and that name goes a long way in perception as well. While there are perhaps thousands of boards that might perform equally to the category leaders, it takes more than what is inside the box to sell the box.

If every brand was able to perform a blind taste test, how would you stack up to the competition? Could your basement brew match up with *Coors* or *Budweiser* who make many, many millions in revenue? Would your small line of apparel outmatch *Reebok* or *Nike* if the logos were removed? There are established brands that have big names and big budgets, and probably a big head start.

But, if you are confident that you have the ideal concept, product, strategy, event, or proposal and the only reason you have not been able to "take it to the next level" is because of your lack of size (and resources), then it may be time to simply regroup and focus on how you can create a **Puffer Fish** approach.

PUFFER FISH

CASE STUDY

SPORT SPECIFIC PERFORMANCE

We launched *Sport Specific Performance,* an all-natural line of golf supplements targeting the weekend warrior that didn't exercise or take vitamins or supplements. While our product was sound and our concept was very well received, we had a huge problem... a small bottom line. We had literally no money in our budget beyond R&D, manufacturing, packaging, and some simple collateral materials. We needed to find a way to promote the brand and drive revenue when we didn't have the advertising budget or the slotting/support fees that most retailers required.

What we did have (having worked in the sports marketing industry for years) was access to **Starfish** (celebrity talent) and the knowledge that **Environmentalists** (philanthropy) and golf were soft spots for a majority of famous people. And if we could find a way to incorporate celebrity star power organically into our line, we could create a campaign that did not have celebrity endorsements per se, but still allowed us to capitalize on their fame to promote the brand.

We created the *Sport Specific Performance* web show on *Ubroadcast.com* that performed live at various celebrity golf events, charity dinners, etc. where we would provide our visibility and media in return for access to a significant list of talent. Our **Puffer Fish** strategy was to appear like *ESPN* when we were really little more than a common *YouTube* user. Before we knew it, we were receiving requests to have our show attend events, promote the charities with press releases and interview teases, and interview such icons as Nick Lachey, Michael Chiklis, Jerry Rice, Drew Brees, and dozens more as our *Sport Specific Performance* banners hung as a set backdrop!

With our viral (and **Puffer Fish** budget friendly) campaign, we promoted the program featuring sought after names that fans would *Google* including Donavan McNabb, Ray Romano, and others.

Along the way, we allowed celebrities a forum to promote their charities while simultaneously conducting our show to put *Sport Specific Performance* on the map!

Everyone wants to be the next big thing. Even the next big thing wants to be a bigger thing than the thing they are. It's the basic economic conundrum of always growing. Increase market share, increase sales, and increase revenue. No one says, *"I hope to keep my fledgling brand at a barely survivable level."* But with limited resources and increased competition, how can smaller marketing personnel compete with the juggernauts at the blue chip companies that have more employees in the mail room than you have altogether? **Puffer Fish**.

In today's landscape with technology engrained in practically every consumer's day-to-day existence, the digital age can be very accommodating to a small fish trying to grow. A good, sound website that achieves the right balance of sizzle, content, practicality, and usefulness can make small fish appear big and neutralize the advances of the big fish that would eat you alive in an open ocean.

The number one question I get when discussing my

agency to clients or peers (aside from "how many *Diet Cokes* are you on right now?") is how big are you? I know when someone asks me this, 99% of the time what they are expressing is really, *"Wow, the amount of work you produce and the quality of your activations are very professional and must have an army of marketing MBAs at the helm".* I know this because having had that conversation at times, I often find potential clients concerned that my group might be *too big* and thus too expensive for their marketing budget. I look around at the half-dozen employees of LONGBOARD Marketing and laugh out loud every time. Imagine spending time as a boutique agency telling customers you are *not* as big as you look and will give them the undivided attention they deserve! Good problem to have, right?

In fact, we often sell ourselves to the limit of our resources (and maybe once or twice a little beyond our maximum bandwidth) but we never fail to exceed expectations by providing better creative, passion, and effort than the much bigger competitors. We may be small in stature, but we are more nimble, more dynamic, and frankly with smaller overhead, we can operate at less cost than the other guys. As long as our agency's DNA of unsurpassed creative thinking and intense passion are able to be seen in every activation, we don't worry about the scope or size of the project.

Every small *Facebook* project and every large 25-city celebrity tour feature our hallmark creative concepts that set us apart from the competition.

We owe a significant portion of our success to applying the **Puffer Fish** strategy digitally. While I may be biased, I would put our creative concepts and digital design up against anyone else's. I always say creativity is free, yet priceless. So if you have a vehicle to communicate your effort across a level playing field, then you have no one to blame but yourself if you don't succeed.

If you and your brand were a painting, and your market was a gallery, how would you do? If customers viewed your product without bias, without favor, without size or placement advantage, what would they say? If you paddled out into a set of waves on a standard size board with anonymous surfers, would you get the best ride? Simply put, strip away the *Nike* swoosh off the shirt and the fancy *Jaguar* showroom away from the car and the toys out of the *Happy Meals* and tell me if the consumer would still appreciate your painting the most.

Until the last few decades, we never had a level playing field to road test brands like the Internet provides. Grocery stores have a whole hierarchy of brand placement and shelf slotting, car manufactures spend millions on lobbyists to create favorable laws, and big-time companies churn out big-time marketing and advertising campaigns with budgets that would make the average brand cringe. The small, 400 sq. ft. corner boutique can't compete next to *Nordstrom* on a city block but if all of the different companies were forced into the same generic space and forced to compete on a more level field, would things be different? The digital space allows fifteen-year-old kids to design sites that give the impression that it was the handy work of a seasoned ad agency pro. Good design, smart messaging, and sizzle can mask the true size of a product, brand, or company. And that's the mantra of the **Puffer Fish**. Look big and act big even if you may not be as robust as you wish to be.

We are very conscientious to make sure our website is dynamic, creative, and full of nuggets that provide a glimpse into the product or service you get with us. It allows us to instantly communicate our brand and or company's philosophy. It neutralizes the department store mannequins, the shiny 10,000-foot retail shopping floor, or the $2 million price tag of the thirty-second Super Bowl spot.

Time and time again, I tell clients that a **Puffer Fish's** number one strength in looking bigger today is a sound website and digital strategy, plain and simple. You can show character, communicate features and benefits, and cost-effectively sell your wares for the price of a *Go*

Daddy domain name and small hosting fee. (Of course web programming, bandwidth, servers, e-commerce, etc. increase costs but you get the point). Our mission at LONGBOARD Marketing was to out-creative the competition and provide the passion of our team on every job we do. That was our competitive advantage and by designing a site that expressed our culture and reflected examples of our promise, we were able to attract the type of clients that we could have never worked with had we been doing this in 1994.

Our use of talent (we discuss talent extensively in the STARFISH chapter) and the ability to showcase some of our creative tours, award-winning promotions, and various campaigns in a fast-paced, excited package of animation, still images, video, etc. makes for a very compelling resource that does the selling for us. While I'm quite confident we spent a fraction of the resources that say *ford.com* or *geico.com* put into their products, I would say with bias that we are right there in the final result. The web provides the how but you still need sound communication, precise messaging, and interesting storytelling to communicate your "why".

To put it in a surfing analogy, the Internet makes conditions a clear, calm flat day with no surf. Laird Hamilton would laugh me out of the water if we both tried to catch the same fifteen-foot wave but if there is absolutely no surf, how would you know that Kelly

Slater or Hamilton were that much better than me if we just sat bobbing on our boards? I can honestly say that I would be a much more equal surfer to the guys on the ASP tour if the contest took place in the bay with no surf.

Once the subjective elements have been equalized, your brand can rely on the variables that set you apart whether it is price, quality, or other variables that you communicate. You will always battle trying to drive e-commerce against *Amazon* or *Costco* and other services that get a much better bulk-rate for inventory but unless your model is driving sales on your site, you can equalize it dramatically utilizing the digital tricks that we cyber **Puffer Fish** deploy.

As a caveat to utilizing the web to drive your branding, I must take a minute and express that, while a sound microsite can be a great tool for the smaller guy, it is not a *"Field of Dreams"*. If you build it, they will *not* always come. I have clients that often say, *"Let's create a great site and we'll have millions of hits by the close of business."* I wish it were that simple but a great site alone does not ensure success.

A **Puffer Fish** can maximize its appearance and indeed drive incrementally more business than the resources provide, but there are still factors that limit the smaller guy. *Google* ads, banners, paid media, and so on will always provide a competitive advantage and sometimes, even the best sites go unnoticed. Building a great site is not the stand-alone tactic for success just as a certain board or goofy-foot style is a sure thing to win a surfing tournament. I simply believe and have proven that a strong website that clearly provides a positive experience for current and potential customers utilizing truly innovative and engaging content can provide a smaller player with an incrementally larger presence. Combine a good solid, professionally designed site with sound marketing and promotion and you can indeed create a strategy that maximizes limited resources. While we could spend hours about key words and tags, it goes without saying that the site needs to have SEO components integrated into the site and sound search elements beyond a great idea.

Another area to address here is the viral aspect of user shared content. I have had clients tell us to *"create a funny, viral video and we'll get millions of impressions." Sounds* simple, right?

While there are cases of an overnight sensation being born in cyberspace (Didn't Justin Bieber get discovered via *YouTube*?) I never subscribe to the lottery approach of hoping a kitty playing piano video is going to make your product a household name. It's the farthest thing from a sure thing but there are ways to incrementally grow using the vehicle. And while we will touch on social media more extensively later in the book, the concept is sound and with emerging social media platforms, a **Puffer Fish** can again exceed their means with well-placed and creative efforts that resonate with users.

PUFFER FISH

SURF LESSON

How Do You Puff-er It?

Take inventory of your best skills, attributes, opportunities, and resources regardless of size or potential. Perform a serious diagnostic of what you have available and if any of the elements can allow you or your brand to "inflate" perception, incrementally gain market share, or provide the perception that you are equal to larger competition. Find what you do better than the competition or what resources you have that can make you stand out and develop that as the core approach. If you don't think that perception is reality, then ask the fine people of *Jack Morton Worldwide* why they lost a multi-million dollar client to a smart-assed surfer like me?

STEP 1: List Your Assets – From tangible resources (like budgets, staff, distribution) to the intangibles that comprise your organization or brand (identifiable brand, edgy attitude, taste, good creative).

STEP 2: Rank Your Assets – If you were on a deserted beach and you treated your list from Step 1 as 1) water, 2) food, 3) shelter, 4) fire, etc., what would be the strongest in order?

STEP 3: Assign A +/- Ratio. – Assign a number to each of the ranked assets. If your Point of Purchase (POP or POS for us marketing vets) routinely wins design awards and is your top marketing resource, then give it +10. If you struggle with a legal department that likes to say "no" more than a nun on the first date, then give it a -10. Once you assign the numbers you can see not only which assets are your strengths, but by how much. Creating a visual scorecard allows you to see the objective elements of a subjective world. When Kelly Slater wins a surfing contest, it's broken down by mathematical score based on the technical elements of a ride: wave size, difficulty of tricks, barrels, etc. That's the only way to accurately score the elements as opposed to rating the entire ride which would mesmerize the judge and influence his opinion.

STEP 4: Swim! – The top strength of your group is the air that inflates the **Puffer Fish**. If you can focus on a key driver, build around it and highlight the features of it beyond the actual component, you exponentially are bigger than that asset. That single greatest asset can be incrementally magnified to produce greater results than the other elements, combined.

If the *GoPro* camera became a phenomenon for action sports enthusiasts based on the strap that fixed it snugly to the surfer, then that point of differentiation should be magnified to separate it from the *Nikons, Flip Videos*, and other cameras currently out there. Hook the top selling point or key characteristic and utilize that as the air that makes your **Puffer Fish** strategy inflate!

Sometimes finding your greatest strength is more difficult than the SURF LESSON and not all of the top ranking elements tell a great story. But, we are marketing people and our goal is to spin a tale that highlights the best components, features, or efforts our brands represent, all in a concise manor. Going back to our core discussion, a **Puffer Fish** approach is not for the weak or the modest. Your goal is to find a nugget that grants you larger than actual size. And once you get that nugget, like a porcupine puffer in the water, you must continue to pump a little hot air around to appear like a bigger fish.

If we look back at the STEP 3 POP example, when great back-cards or shelf materials is your strength, then wouldn't it stand to reason that across both B2B and B2C you maximize that feature? A small garage start-up with professional, attractive POP that wins over consumers is on even footing with the million-dollar POP from a Top 20 CPG company if you don't know who was producing it. Playing up that your POP is unsurpassed in the industry *including* your significantly larger competition takes the focus off of what you lack and puts it on what you do well. So take advantage of that ability and focus your communication on the strengths you bring to the table. Let retailers or potential distributors that along with your brand, you provide the best marketing materials in the industry. Regardless of your budget or size, you can promote the key element of your effort with the same professional results of a much larger fish and thus, activate a bigger-than-we-really-are stance to everyone outside the office who doesn't know you are a just a guppy in a big pond.

PUFFER FISH

CASE STUDY

MEATHEADS

When a top network brought back a reality-style athletic show featuring humongous Meatheads as the stars, they turned to us to create an online effort that would support the return of the pop-culture classic. While the network had an extensive on-air and print strategy already, they wanted to reach the often-cynical 18-24 year old male demographic via a targeted digital campaign. And with limited resources available, we needed to create a large-scale effort on a small-scale budget.

After a long brainstorming session to

create a fun theme that would resonate with the fans, we set about to create a mostly viral effort that would allow our loyal viewers to drive home our messaging. (Nowadays, these crazy kids refer to this as social media/marketing but way back in the dark ages of 2009, it was just viral marketing). Our mission was to exploit the often quirky show elements including how the featured hunks got their crazy names, how fans would look in their huge, buff bodies, and even the cadence and over-the-top pro wrestling-like diatribes the main characters would spew. Once we decided on an overall theme for our digital effort that would encompass these tongue-in-cheek elements, we set about creating an experience that allowed fans to virtually become one of the muscle-bound stars.

Our mission was to create an experience that resonated far beyond the site itself and by allowing fans to engage in the show's phenomenon, they would (in theory) do incrementally more work promoting our show than we could provide in actuality… a perfect *Puffer*

Fish approach of going big on a budget that is rather small. So by creating the *Muscle Messages*, viral videos of the Meatheads doing your dirty work (telling off your boss, breaking up with your spouse, informing a friend that they annoy you, etc.) we allowed fans to engage in the product and send these messages to friends or loved-ones (or maybe not-so-loved ones in this case). With a 10% secondary send rate (people who received a message and then sent another one or visited the site directly from the recipients message to send one) we were able to create a significantly larger campaign with more impressions than we anticipated.

The network campaign was a huge success and served to communicate the new show as well as engage users as to the elements and characters of the program. By having the fans do *our* dirty work reaching out to their contacts (again, all pre-*Facebook*) we were able to deliver a campaign that was incrementally larger in scale and results than the budget or resources should have allowed for.

Humorist Malcolm Gladwell wrote in his book *"The Tipping Point"* that there are a certain amount of *Influencers* who can lead a larger group to action. His theory is that a small, hip group of trend setters can direct the masses and it's actually very much the main force behind both the surfing culture and the **Puffer Fish** strategy. When a good surfer or a 'cool kid' from school busts out a new brand, piece of equipment, etc. then it instantly has a credibility factor.

The **Puffer Fish** relies significantly on the influence of others and word-of-mouth to accomplish its mission. Even if you set yourself up to appear larger, create dynamic digital and social arms to build interest, and follow this chapter step by step, you still need to have those people out there who pollinate the masses. It could be a single happy client, a small article in a magazine, or a celebrity eating your product but it takes a spark to start a fire.

Reaching those in the know, those who can direct the millions of followers, and being the lead surfer in the pack is a key way for a small brand to go from ankle-slapper to tsunami. Sometimes this **Puffer Fish** approach works and sometimes it fails to ignite. But when influential consumers and authorities promote your brand, you can incrementally reach far more of the masses than you initially accounted for.

PUFFER FISH

CASE STUDY

ZICO WINS THE RACE!

The Surfer's Guide To Marketing looks to bring surf, beach, and nautical references to the marketing conversation and I actively sought out cool, smart "beach" brands to help showcase the lessons presented. *ZICO Coconut Water* is a natural beverage full of electrolytes and potassium and comes in great flavors. It's a favorite of athletes everywhere for the ability to replenish valuable nutrients lost while exercising. And it tastes way better than the gallons of salt water I ingest every time I hit the surf!

With limited budgets, *ZICO* wanted to have a presence at some of the biggest athletic participation events in America like the New York Marathon and the *ZICO* team set their sights on winning the race... the marketing race. While

Gatorade and other water companies paid in the high six figures to sponsor the event, *ZICO* took the **Puffer Fish** approach once they had permission to just be on-site.

With a guerrilla presence at the race, rather than just hit the attendees, the *ZICO* staff supplied the various event workers with cases of free *ZICO* water as well. The booths selling clothing, the shoe experts, the race massage booth, etc. all had unlimited free *ZICO* to consume during the race. The team of **Puffer Fish** then positioned themselves at the finish and were quick to offer the elite level runners free *ZICO* when they crossed the line. Now for those of you who have run 26.2 miles, you know that you will drink pretty much anything after hours of non-stop running. And when *ZICO* was there on the spot, they were positively received by the tired athletes.

Now flash forward as the "civilian" non-elite runners begin to meander across the line and they see all the pros drinking their beverage. They glance at all the staffers drinking *ZICO*. Who wants to be left out of the party, right?

So while *Gatorade* and other drinks paid a significant amount of money to have their brand hanging on the banners, *ZICO* slipped in and had their brand being used by hard-core racers, support staff, and casual runners alike. After that, the crowd looked at the other drinks who wasted tons of money on signage as, well (coco)nuts!

I love to showcase examples of small groups utilizing limited resources to drive their business. The *ZICO* case shows that a lot of elbow grease and a little luck can allow you to create a presence. It's about being smart, creative, and tactical. The core of the **Puffer Fish** approach is centered on effort and what you lack in resource, you make up in sweat equity.

Want another example of how you can establish your brand on a limited budget? You're holding it. Utilize your experience, industry knowledge, or persuasive talents to become an "expert" in the field to drive your brand.

Let's be honest, you had never heard of me, my agency, or some of the work I've discussed. But, you might have "Googled" *The Surfer's Guide To Marketing*, Randy Rovegno, or LONGBOARD Marketing to make sure that you weren't throwing away your money on yet another boring marketing overview. And that's free promotional support!

Becoming an expert isn't hard as long as you have some experience and an opinion. How many of us have gone to conferences or trade shows to hear panelists basically convey the same opinion as everyone else? Or read an op-ed piece in your trade pub? Searched for a blog with interesting tidbits from one of your peers? By becoming a writer, expert, and/or spokesman, you build instant visibility and can promote your product or service to the masses.

With today' digital algorithms, your company should have multiple touch points to establish a digital footprint and you can create content to drive search elements while simultaneously becoming the expert in the field. Maintain a blog, vlog, and the usual social media outlets and be sure to keep them current and robust. Speak on panels. Provide quotes to newspapers/media for relevant happenings in your community. Write articles in your trade pubs or for business websites. The key to becoming an expert and gaining valuable exposure for your brand is to have a combination of a sound bio/resume (For mine, along with brands I've championed like *ESPN* and *AT&T*, I have college lecturer, panelist, and now author) and a constant and current voice. The more your brand is out there, the more likely consumers or clients are to run across you.

As a true **Puffer Fish** who does more with less, it is without a doubt an asset to be an authority, have a sound opinion and in the absence of a strong budget, have your good name and reputation to serve as collateral to vouch for your brand. Remember, it's about appearing bigger, better, and more robust and if there is an "expert" (or witty marketer turned wannabe surfer turned author) at the helm, it gives you credibility. If you are going to swim like a **Puffer Fish**, you might as well become an expert **Puffer Fish**!

"Surfing is a special kind of madness, a feeling for the sea, a combination of love, knowledge, respect, fear- instinctive perception gained through repeated contact."

- Tom Curren

CHAPTER 2

BARNACLE

You don't need to be Jacques Cousteau to know about the barnacle. These little sea critters latch on to a larger object and ride out the tides attached to their host. These smaller animals are the acne on a whale's mug and they utilize their larger host to allow them to survive and flourish. The pier, the swimming whale, or ocean rock that the little mollusk attaches to offers them security and a home-base while they proceed to eat, reproduce, and do whatever the hell barnacles do.

This one-way opportunity allows for a simple chance to get in the game without all of the efforts to create the game. It may cost money or other consideration but generally the price of entry is lighter than the value you will provide. While certain brands may bring credibility, awareness, or even a fun and desirable concept for the activation, generally the *Barnacle* is more of a *Puffer Fish* looking for a home to attach to.

The key to executing a successful *Barnacle* approach is to simply be perceived as value-add. There are a few key assumptions to determine if the *Barnacle* tactic is right approach and is seen as a cost-effective opportunity to join the feeding frenzy or simply a freeloader trying to get a lift from reef to reef.

It should be determined if the existing event, experience, or effort is already good-to-go and your presence is not a factor in the success or failure. The carnival is coming to town regardless and completely self-contained whether your sampling team or display is there or not. In fact, some may argue that adding your presence is a hindrance and detrimental to the existing activation, especially if you are not contributing much in the way of logistics, demand, or financial input. When a good surfer paddles out to a break where you have already been surfing, it could be seen as a positive in terms of having some company. Or while maybe being able to watch a guy who can really shred or pull off some good moves is a plus, ultimately you know that his presence could limit *your* access to waves or cut down on your own effectiveness as he's going to take a piece of your pie. There are both advantages and disadvantages and it's simply a combination of true value meets perceived value. Hopefully, you front enough to give that impression without paying fair market value.

If you have done many events or promotions, you probably have been some form of a **Barnacle**, or more than likely, been approached by someone trying to ride *your* coattails as one. Utilizing someone else's work or presence to promote your own existence is a simple and cost-effective way to advance your organization. When large-scale events, carnivals, sporting arenas, etc. put on their various local fairs, farmers markets, or live games, they need sponsors to help fund their activities and thus provide signage or space for their partners.   They promote the event and the sponsors help pay for it (see more about the **Remora** for 50/50 partnerships)

As a surfer, you don't want to spend all of your energy paddling around if you can position yourself to allow for only a few strokes to catch the wave. And if there is a current that helps pull you out into the lineup versus fighting your way against the white water, you take advantage of that as well. The less work or effort required to accomplish your goal, the better. It seems like an easy theory to uphold but too often, marketing groups will want to own the entire activity rather than be one of the cogs in the machine. That requires incremental costs and resources and definitely isn't floating out to sea via the moving tide.

If you can simply glom on to someone else's existing event or effort and receive the traffic, impressions, and exposure at a fraction of the resources, then you are a **Barnacle**! To be clear, I am not suggesting that you lose your identity, give in to unreasonable demands, or even latch on to an event that is not ideal simply because it is available. Rather, look at a multitude of events that align with your brand or objective and see where you can add your name without burning through a disproportionate amount of your funds or manpower.

There are several schools of thought in terms of associating with an existing campaign and it's not always a black-and-white decision. While some partnerships are more symbiotic (see the REMORA chapter), you need to make sure that there is indeed a strong benefit to the **Barnacle** and not much needed in return. Sometimes even the smallest fees of entry or requirements might not be worth it. Sometimes you can find an event or opportunity that despite a small or insignificant requirement to attend or partner with still isn't worth the minimal attendance or impact and thus, no matter how inexpensive, is still not a valuable proposition.

The key factor when going into an effort as a **Barnacle** includes a lack of resources to create, own, or control the opportunity yourself. Simply put, if you had the money and resources, could you build, advertise, and activate your own stand-alone campaign? Not relying on other groups, agencies, properties, etc. is a huge advantage if all things were equal and I always say that if the budget and parameters allow you to properly do a stand-alone activation then by all means, own it! (We discuss this approach later featuring the *Wahoo's Fish Tacos* CASE STUDY later in the book).

Frankly, if you are expecting to be included in someone else's campaign by paying little to no compensation, then you're probably going to endure incremental steps and many Kahunas telling you what and how you can associate with their event.

Sometimes groups that may have enjoyed the opportunity to participate at a lower entry point find themselves ultimately being subjected to increased costs or a greater effort to partner than they originally anticipated. In fact, the initial price that appeared like a good deal has suddenly cost you more than doing it yourself. Shopping Malls, City Squares, etc. are notorious for quoting one price and then "adding" variables that cost you more. We have done athlete autograph signings at malls where, after a small inclusion fee to be part of their all-store sale weekend event, suddenly hit us with extra chargers for electricity (outlets) extra security, and even mall administrative fees. While I'm not saying they are used car salesmen adding undercoating costs, I just want to ensure that the deal you negotiate as a *Barnacle* is favorable and you don't end up spending more on a low-budget partnership than you expected.

The other key factor in successfully becoming a *Barnacle* is to bring so much (perceived) value to the existing event that they *have* to say "*yes*". The whale that has barnacles all over his chin must think it looks cool in the aquatic mammal world and thus lets them stick around. The same philosophy and attitude is a powerful tool for the *Barnacle* and the approach is paramount. Reaching out to a potential host and saying that you don't have much money but want to draw *their* customers to your booth probably isn't going to be a successful approach. But telling a fantastic version of your brand or offer and providing features and benefits "allowing" them to share in your glory is a great approach to help turn the tides. Remember, we do bring *some* value, just not *equal* value.

When I do events or large-scale activations, anything we advertise brings out consumers, media... and **Barnacles!** Guerrilla marketing thrives at the expense of others and I would never show up at someone's event without coordinating first and "officially" becoming a partner or participant. Crashing a party is a no-no and I don't want to be a bush-league agency that arrives uninvited. The strippers that pass out flyers for their strip club after sporting events are not, in my opinion, considered **Barnacles,** rather skanky, dirty, wannabe **Barnacles.** They have the basic philosophy down by latching on to the game's traffic and taking advantage of the crowds generated from someone else but they are not brining even a little value to their host.

It doesn't need to be 50/50 (that's a **Remora**) but you have to bring *some* semblance of value to the host. Guerrilla marketers that pass out flyers to your crowd are not bringing anything to the table so please don't think I condone that behavior. Whenever we do street teams in different areas, we work with the host, explain our goals and objectives, and provide some form of value, from demonstrations to coupons to free premiums. In other words, something that validates why we are serving as **Barnacles.**

As a marketer, we are all required to have a little salesmanship, or even showmanship, in our skill set. You probably argue, errrr... *discuss* with peers or management about adding elements to the product that affects the P&L or strongly persuade a client that your marketing campaign will be the most successful tool to reach their goal. Or perhaps when fighting for a career-advancing promotion, I doubt you start off by saying that you have been stealing office pens and spending hours a day on *Facebook* at work. Frame the story so it's in the best light and that your addition to the existing campaign is a huge asset to *them*.

As a soul surfer and aspiring man of fortitude, I will *never* lie or mislead my clients, partners or vendors. While I have been lied to or sold a story that the teller cannot deliver, my approach has always been to simply accent the positives and make sure the greatest selling points and value significantly offset the drawbacks and red flags.

Just as it's our job to communicate the best attributes of a product or service, you can also enhance the pitch by *not* saying things. I see *Mountain Dew* spots talk about refreshing taste and enjoyment. I never see them say that it's the result of Phosphoric Acid, Aspartame, and Potassium Benzoate. Are they lying by not including that? Certainly not, but I doubt the first words out of any realtor's mouth when showing a property is how many people were murdered in the place. So when they *have* to announce their shortcomings or warts as the pharmaceutical industry is required to, I'm surprised anyone tries the drugs at all. (Besides, what symptoms do you have that are worse than the long list of side effects they mention including anal leakage, amnesia, and bleeding eyes?!)

I call some agency pitches *"Singing Purple Elephants"* because they will look you in the eye and swear they can get you the talented, off-color pachyderm if you give them the business. And guess what happens once you sign the agreement... they stare at you dumfounded when you ask for your *"Singing Purple Elephant"*!

As an incredibly creative thinker (see the chapter on TOW-IN SURFING about creative approaches to marketing) I may not be able to match my SAT score with some of the brilliant marketing minds in our industry (or the average American for that matter) but I would put our group's creative brilliance up against anyone. When I put on my Lucy Ricardo wig and come up with a hair-brained scheme to do something that has never been done before, we always do our homework to ensure that the pitch is indeed doable. It's one thing to wish to fly, but it's another thing entirely to claim you can fly without having wings. Dream the impossible, but make sure you can actually get there when push comes to shove.

Many times I have been asked what one of my favorite professional moments has been and I vividly remember a day in December a few years back where I was working feverishly on two separate RFPs (Request For Proposal for all of you non-marketing rhetoric speakers) for unique clients. For the premiere of a television network's new primetime outdoor show, we had a great concept that required a unique wilderness activation… complete with a live 1,000 pound grizzly bear (don't ask!). Simultaneously, we were putting the finishing touches on another client's holiday pitch where we were going to do a unique Times Square activation in New York complete with Santa Claus, premiums in the form of free presents, and a host of elves. Before finalizing the proposals, I did my usual due diligence and in a matter of hours had confirmed the availability, logistics, and pricing for a real life grizzly bear and a few dozen little people to perform. What a day…. bears and midgets! Gosh, I love LA.

The whole point of my story, aside from the fact that I now have bears and little people on speed dial, is that while you should always believe in your concepts, support it with proven research. Leave nothing to chance or the unexpected. And feel confident that when you communicate the various elements of your story, they are doable. While it's Sales 101, I need to reinforce that the proper attitude and approach is half of the battle because after all, **Barnacles** are basically asking to get something for almost nothing. So give the brand the confidence that the tangibility of your activation will bring the concept to life. Whether you are selling in an idea as an agency, a marketing exec explaining the concept to senior leaders, or even getting buy off from the board, marketers are always selling in the big idea and it makes it easier when you have the support to back it up.

The offer needs to be compelling enough to garner a vote of confidence when really by all account, you are a salmon swimming upstream. There is nothing more satisfying when, after working the room with visions of huge animals and tiny humans, the client stares back with wide-eyes, and open mouth, and asks if you really can fulfill this amazing opportunity. When they stop looking at what you are presenting and start asking about the details or logistics of how you could possibly produce the impossible, you've got the business!

Selling in a brilliant concept is half the battle. The execution is the other half. The ability to come up with good ideas and the experience to engage techniques to make it come to fruition is a balance that will set you apart. Good idea + mediocre execution = bad results. Average idea + good execution = fair results. But being good at all phases of the game = success!

This chapter involves discussing one of my proven techniques, the **Barnacle** to accomplish the big idea with limited resources. The basics that we've discussed highlight the ability to take a smaller scale entity and latch on to a larger property to thrive in the open ocean. The way to frame the story as well as the opportunities to secure an ideal "whale" are all integral parts of the mix.

To become a **Barnacle** at a local mall event or festival, I might bring the sizzle so they buy the steak when they didn't even know they were hungry. While George Costanza of *Seinfeld* fame lives by the credo *"It's not a lie if you believe it,"* I tend to simply emphasize the value of what we can bring and downplay what we would ask for in return.

BARNACLE

SURF LESSON

HANG A STAR ON THAT ONE

Any instructor giving you surfing lessons (especially if it's your first time) will tell you step-by-step how to get in position, paddle, and stand up. Executing these maneuvers is easier said than done. But, once you start to get up a few times, feel your own balance, and gain a little confidence and experience, you can take the surf lesson and grow from it. *The Surfer's Guide To Marketing* SURF LESSONS are the same way; showing you how we have successfully navigated the various opportunities we are discussing and allowing you to create your own version to find which surfing stance works best for you.

In the case of presenting the *Barnacle* strategy when you really don't have as much to offer as you are trying to receive in return, I often focus on the single aspect of the pitch that has some sizzle and stick to highlighting that as the benefit for the host that we are attempting to latch on to. A sample of my approach to be included in an existing event that is already well-promoted, farther along in the development process, and generally not relying on my additional elements to make it thrive might be as follows;

"Hello, we have an amazing opportunity to have our famous celebrity athlete Starfish attend your event. We have

done numerous appearances similar to what you are doing and customers walk away thrilled with the opportunity to meet a famous athlete like Bobby Barnacle. In fact, along with having Mr. Barnacle on-site signing autographs and meeting the fans, we could even bring some of our attractive Brand Ambassadors to distribute free premiums."

At this point, the host event producer tends to think we are going to ask for fees for the integration of our player or Brand Ambassadors when in reality, we simply want to activate our effort without paying their on-site fees, sponsorship, etc. They usually will ask if they have to provide any money or what the requirements on their end will be in order to get such an "unbelievable" deal.

"We actually have some surplus premium items and a contractual appearance with Mr. Barnacle based on our previous agreement so in reality, in won't cost you anything. As I mentioned earlier, we actually have done several similar successful activations so we are completely self-contained. All we would

need from you is a space, preferably in a high-traffic location where people can see Mr. Barnacle at your event. And of course, to ensure you get the maximum exposure from us bringing our talent, you should incorporate Mr. Barnacle's appearance (presented by Brand X of course) into as much of your media and promotions as possible to help you drive your traffic. And that's pretty much it for your end as we will bring the signage, tents, Brand Ambassadors and support staff and even free giveaways."

It's simply a much more positive approach than saying you want to bring a booth, promote your brands, give away your items to their customers, and oh yeah… have them advertise your brand while you don't pay you anything to be there.

A lot of our clients want to be the **Barnacle** at other events and we are constantly searching local markets' calendar of events for the right partnerships. It's our goal to find an opportunity to provide value-add for the event while providing exposure for the client that wants to be involved. While there are hundreds of events in different markers around the country, finding the ideal fit to maximize your effort needs to be a key focus. It goes without saying that an AYSO youth soccer tournament that draws an estimated 25,000 people still isn't a good host for a *Budweiser* **Barnacle** attempt. But the same activation with *Nike* might be a much better fit. It may sound obvious to make sure your events are a good fit with your brand but there have been times when we have had clients ask to be at affairs that made no sense and had us pretty much a fish out of water.

BARNACLE

CASE STUDY

THE BIG GAME

The biggest event in the United States every year is the Super Bowl. As a marketer, it's the big leagues in terms of scale, cost, and exposure (see the chapter on **Big Waves**). Ad time in the game costs seven-figures for a thirty-second spot and sponsorship of various official Super Bowl elements are a huge investment. So creating your own Super Bowl event that cuts through the clutter and stands out among literally hundreds of events is a costly and extensive undertaking.

So when our client wanted to be part of the action of the Super Bowl, they approached us with the ultimate opportunity to demonstrate our *Barnacle* philosophy and latch on to someone else's huge efforts. For Super Bowl XLV in Dallas, our mission was to create a presence for our client at the big game in Big D.... but without the hefty price tag or reasonable lead time. After all, creating an engaging experience that competes with the biggest spectacle in sports without all of the pesky budget or months of preparation is what every marketing veteran lives for, right? But as the saying goes, *"Go big or go home."*

When our client's major sports partner announced that they were going to be broadcasting all of their television and radio shows from a local mall in nearby Fort Worth, including all of their talent-filled programs, we took this as an opportunity to drive awareness and branding without having to reinvent the wheel and create the event itself. This weeklong festival would attract hundreds of thousands of passionate fans and it was simply our job to carve out a place on the reef to get our share of plankton.

So in an expedited manor, we secured space and created the Digital Living Room activation that accented the various broadcasts and events throughout the week. Our interactive booth would allow fans to experience our outdoor living room complete with sofas, tables, chairs, rugs, multiple flat screens showing the network's programming in HD and 3D, broadband displays, and tons of branded premiums all promoting how our client and its partnerships were the only option for sports fans. Add to that our beautiful Brand Ambassadors and *Starfish* appearances from Hall of Fame RB Eric Dickerson, former All Pro RB Christian "The Nigerian Nightmare" Okoye, and three-time Super Bowl Champion Roger Craig and we had an attractive booth that held its own with the existing large-scale production.

While some brands spend millions

creating their own Super Bowl event including the *Bud Light* Hotel, *DIRECTV's* Beach Bash, and more, we were able to reach thousands of passionate Super Bowl fans attending the shopping center's events as a complement to the host network. While our Digital Living Room was a component of the bigger picture, we served as a supporting actor to the main event and even provided value-add to their experience. And in so doing, saved our client significant dollars playing the role of the **Barnacle** attaching to the existing event and the crowds they generated.

Editors Note: As mentioned previously, surfers are the ultimate optimists and make lemonade whenever presented with lemons. So when the 2011 Dallas/Ft. Worth Super Bowl week was hit with "the storm of the century" including wind, snow, and -5 degree temperatures, our outdoor living room seemed like a disaster in the making. But, a few quick adjustments (and several large space heaters later) our virtual living room became a shelter from the elements for the crazy fans that still braved the cold. While we had to endure some good natured ribbing for the unfortunate circumstances (including comments that our living room was "just like the fan's own homes...only with five inches of snow inside", or people wanting to tell Christian Okoye to change his nickname to "The *Siberian* Nightmare", we still exhausted our inventory of client literature and branded premiums representing the maximum quantity of impressions we were targeting!

There are a multitude of existing locations or properties that a **Barnacle** would thrive in. Most often, the "mall tour" seems to be a quick fix for the on-location event. Because of the diverse nature of shopping centers and the space and familiarity of this type of marketing effort, we often find that shopping centers or outdoor plazas are very receptive to hosting events. If your opportunity allows for co-branded advertising or mentions of the location, you can leverage the partnership even more. But I tell clients to try not to think within the proverbial box, as a good **Barnacle** doesn't always need to be attached to a big pier to survive. There are reefs, rocks, fish, sunken ships, etc. that can serve as a great home for your needs so don't get too caught up in one of the traditional avenues.

We recently did an activation in an airport for a client and found that the campaign was a huge success. After reviewing the demographics of a traveler, we found that they match up ideally to the upscale or affluent demographic we were seeking. We discovered the average traveler's household income was well above average and a ridiculously high amount (in excess of 70%) are college educated. Add to that the average down time of an airport traveler at the facility was thirty minutes and we have a formula for huge marketing results. You give me financially secure, confined, intelligent consumers and I'll show you a demographic that will purchase goods and services.

Perhaps your business solutions software wants to reach Fortune 500 companies or your golf line that caters to senior level nine-to-fivers is looking to market to the professional crowd. I suggest looking at the jet-set road warriors and see if you can create a unique marketing opportunity in a desirable space that, no pun intended, tend to fly under the marketing radar. They are bored to tears in the terminal and will demo your clubs, sign up for your service, or visit your link in an effort to stave off the doldrums of travel.

All of these past examples showcase how your brand can become a **Barnacle** and attach to an existing campaign at significantly less cost than creating it yourself. The keys to pulling off a **Barnacle** (which is an ironic use of terms since the goal is to stick around) is to ensure that your cost of entry is minimal, the results exceed what you would garner if you paid, and while you may disproportionately benefit from your host, you still bring some value. So now you know of venues and platforms you can attach to, techniques to best position your unbalanced offer, and different points to look for. So become a **Barnacle**, increase your benefits, and succeed! Just don't attach yourself to my activations!

"Surfing, alone among sports, generates laughter at its very suggestion, and this is because it turns not a skill into an art, but an inexplicable and useless urge into a vital way of life."

- Matt Warshaw

CHAPTER 3

REMORA

If the *Barnacle* approach is adding yourself into an existing lineup and paddling out to where a dozen surfers have already set up shop where you don't bring much value, then the *Remora* is going to a new break with a few of your mates and paddling out together. It's much more of a 50/50 relationship. A *Barnacle* doesn't provide much for the host in return for being able to latch on to the larger partner's effort but a **Remora** approach is more of a win-win. It's a classic version where your goods/services match any partner's efforts and you both see the opportunity as positive.

When a larger sea animal like a whale or a shark needs a partner, they look no further than the remora. The suckerfish attaches to the larger host and proceeds to eat the various microorganisms, fungus, or algae from their counterpart's body. The symbiotic relationship benefits both parties as the host fish gets a free cleaning while the remora gets a free meal. Both animals prosper.

There are countless opportunities for a marketer to create a successful partnership using the **Remora** approach. Different from the **Barnacle** where one partner provides the majority of the benefits, becoming a **Remora** requires elements from both partners to make for a successful effort. Athletes tend to be ideal partners for a **Remora** to approach if you have an athletic apparel line, sneaker or relevant sports equipment that they can showcase.

Players need to wear shoes or cleats depending on their sport so *Nike, Reebok, Under Armour* and all of the sneaker companies spend millions to create a win-win relationship. Michael Jordan wore *Nike* and

millions of fans wanted to *"Be Like Mike"*. He gets paid
to wear the product (the tools of his trade) and in return,
he provides credibility and exposure for the brand.
(There's more on the use of talent in the chapter on
STARFISH.) Add to it another symbiotic level when
Nike puts him in commercials and you now have a very
well-paid spokesmen providing testimonial for how
great your product is.

Surfers and athletes in general tend to be very
particular about their equipment and prefer certain
brands or models. But having said that, the majority of
athletes either directly or indirectly participate in the
Remora tactic every time they paddle out, hit a homer,
or score a goal. And while they claim they like a certain
style or model, it's surprising how well they can adapt to
a new brand if there is a check behind the move.

It's a mutually beneficial opportunity that requires both
parties to bring resources to the table and along with
traditional examples, I often encourage my peers to
seek out new partnerships and logical tie-ins that have
not be exploited. Traditional channels and partnerships
are not a negative and in fact are the tried-and-true
backbone of an organization. But I hate to do the
expected 100% of the time. It's ok to have a
percentage of your business tied in with traditional
partnerships but always looking for new, innovative,
and often unpredictable partnerships can have an

incremental impact on a brand by adding an eye-opening freshness to the mix.

For example, a local radio station bringing their remote broadcast to your event is a classic **Remora** move. The event provides the story, the location, and the reason for being while the radio remote gets to cover the occasion in return for providing exposure. While some radio stations will also want to be compensated for their time/effort based on the overall reach and impressions they provide, my experience has been that if you can provide unique opportunities for them including exclusive content that will bring value, etc. then let them **Remora** up and latch on to your event! I find that allowing local stations access to the **Starfish** talent your event features or tickets to give away to their listeners often serves as a fair balance. Or to make it a *Surfer's Guide* term... (s)*quid pro quo*.

One thing to note when finding a broadcast partner is to ensure that they fit the demographic. Your local sports radio station might not be very interested in doing a remote for the local bridal expo. While it sounds obvious, I have had more than one client look at the overall GRPs or impressions rather than looking at the demographics. Now, if you are working at a local game or sports-related theme and the male demographics from a Country Music station align similarly to the local AM sports talk station, and you can garner significantly more impressions for the same *Remora* proposition, then you may want to consider it. Logically, you think sports talk but look deeper and see if an ideal male demo with twice as many listeners might not just be better.   Time and time again, I have found that like-attracts-like and even if you sacrifice total impressions with a larger reaching station that isn't your prime association, you may produce a better on-brand experience and ultimately benefit more. Just do your homework before you buy.

Always ensure that the partnership you form with your *Remora* counterpart is sweet enough for both ends and that aside from the on-site remote, you get "X" amount of mentions, updates on their events web page, and testimonial from their on-air broadcast talent. Whatever your equation is worth, a true partnership offers as much food for the remora as cleanliness for the host shark. Don't do it unless you both prosper.

There are several considerations when choosing to adopt a *Remora* strategy including selection of the right host, making sure both parties understand the goals or align similarly for the demographic, and both provide equal reciprocation. You need to ensure that, while any advantage that arises will ultimately be yours, you assume that each member in this symbiotic relationship bring a similar mindset, brand, and demographic.

One of the purest forms of a marketing **Remora** is the gift-with-purchase. Brand A offers a free Brand B sample to provide value-add for the host and exposure for the **Remora**. Adding a sample dust cloth with a mop is a prime example. Consumer gets an extra item and exposure to Brand B while Brand A gets incremental sales. Win-win. Remembering that the **Remora** is a split partnership where both parties benefit equally is the key differentiation between this approach and some of the previous discussions.

Larger brands can integrate elements of equally successful products into their product to create more awareness and loyalty as well. When *Orbitz* gum started using *Crest* as a component to whiten teeth, they gained instant credibility. *Crest* toothpaste and teeth whitening products have been around for decades and the added value of the name on the *Orbitz* packaging gives it a strong one-two punch. Both products benefit equally as *Crest* is exposed to the gum chewing crowd and *Orbitz* increases sales with a leader in tooth care as their whitening element.

Intel is a great example of a **Remora** because they partner with computer manufacturers like *Dell*. On all of the ads and packaging for the *Dell* computer, it boasts "featuring the *Intel* Pentium Processor". I don't know what that is but it sounds like I must need it!

It goes without saying that when doing a tie-in or partnership, keeping similar products, services, or demographics involved in the relationship is a given. You would think. I have had clients that, in an effort to push other members of their company's overall portfolio, demand that we give away one product that doesn't really align with the other and I still shake my head at free pair of socks with every purchase of premium vodka promotion I once was presented with.

REMORA

CASE STUDY

FUTBOL

Large consumer facing groups like *GE*, *Proctor & Gamble*, etc. have a wealth of assets and products at their disposal and if all things are equal, supporting a sister division is a great opportunity. With our client's television service provider (a major satellite company) under their corporation's umbrella, the media conglomerate's Spanish language sports networks wanted to drive their demand with the service provider. To create an added incentive for the consumer to purchase the Hispanic Sports package that the service operator was promoting, we created a gift-with-purchase program that the network could present to the partner.

The *Consiga Mas* (Get More) campaign allowed fans who wanted the Spanish language network to earn an added incentive when they subscribed to the provider's package. If the network creating an incentive for their service provider is a **Remora** partnership, then adding yet another element (a third player) is creating a school of **Remoras**!

The third addition to the mix was taking the popular print magazine that accents the network and having the Spanish-language publication provide a six-month free subscription to everyone that signed up for the sports-tier offer featuring our futbol-fanatic client.

The service provider drove their subscriptions with the offer so adding more customers meant more revenue.

The network client was a great partner for the provider by activating the entire promotion and since they are paid for each subscriber that orders their network on the package, they earned more revenue. The magazine was able to increase their circulation numbers to show advertisers as well as provide a sample of their product to their ideal demographic.

The three-way **Remora** strategy was an equal opportunity promotion for all three parties and helped each member succeed in promoting their product while relying on the other(s) to help complete the deal. *Gol! Gol! GOL!*

One of the hardest things for a **Remora** to do is to share. Everyone wants their brand to be the prominent feature in every marketing tactic but remember, a 50-50 split is a victory for this tactic. There are several ways to integrate multiple partners into a campaign or promotion and as long as you all get equal billing, then you are living a symbiotic activation.

Surfers can share waves and there are (usually) plenty to go around. If I catch a nice ride, there is probably another one in the set coming that the next guy can catch. The same general "play nice in the sandbox" philosophy can lead to successful campaigns and produce incrementally greater results that trying to snake all the waves yourself.

Several tactics that can add results by becoming a *Remora* including co-branded direct mail. Instead of using your budget to send 1,000 flyers with your brand exclusively, find an accenting product or service. That way, you can take the joint money and reach 2,000 people with a shared ad. Your line of chips promoted with another group's soda makes for a cost-effective way to double your reach.

If you are sampling a product or holding an event, a good *Remora* brings several non-competing partners to the table. Don't shell out money for food at your retail clothing fashion show if you can get the Mexican Food restaurant to cater it. It's a win-win and crucial to getting more for your budget.

Entertainment companies have long been viewed as *Remoras*. The entire product placement business is based on both partners earning equal value. The movie or TV show requires the use of a vehicle for a scene. Unless it's a specific brand crucial to the plot like the *DeLorean* in *Back to The Future*, most entertainment studios are open to a sponsorship deal providing significant exposure in return for significant compensation. Would *E.T.* not have pretty much been the same movie if that little alien powered through *M&M*'s instead of *Reese's Pieces*?

In this day and age, nothing is left to chance and as long as the watch the hero wears or the clothes are not a period-piece costume, then a brand is selected and agrees to compensate the studio to be a **Remora**. It's a great partnership for both sides and the result is a long-form commercial for the product and in most cases, millions for the filmmaker.

While most of the products in a TV show or movie are not random, rarely does the product truly become a key factor in the episode. But there are examples of going beyond the basic **Remora** agreement as when *NBC's Friends* featured a *Pottery Barn* episode where, beyond the group simply "using" the products from the retailer, the company paid a huge sum to actually be integrated into the plot line. All things considered, it came off as somewhat organic and in the end, people flocked to the retailer to get the same furniture that Rachel and Phoebe discussed on-air.

A true **Remora** will find co-op promotional opportunities and product placement is a great way to get exposure while earning extra revenue. I believe it's a pure example of the **Remora** strategy and as I write this on my super-slick *Mac Book Pro* with the 17" monitor, I sip my cold, refreshing *Diet Coke*, kick up my feet in my size 15 *Reef Smoothy* flip-flops, and listen to amazing music on my *Sirius* satellite radio. Please make your checks payable to Randy Rovegno.

"For those searching for something more than just the norm. We lay it all down, including what others call sanity, for just a few moments on waves larger than life. We do this because we know there is still something greater than all of us. Something that inspires us spiritually. We start going down hill, when we stop taking risks."

- Laird Hamilton

CHAPTER 4

TOW-IN SURFING

While marketing has significant opportunity to evolve and create based on an infinite amount of touch points, expedited in the digital age, we can still look to the lifestyle of surfing to teach us how. Surfing is as basic a sport as there is. You need a board and waves. It's been the same basic concept for hundreds of years.

As *The Surfer's Guide To Marketing* utilizes parallels and surfing examples to explain and evolve marketing principles and strategies, this chapter is dedicated to creativity in the form of the 6'3" waterman and big wave icon Laird Hamilton. He represents creativity, evolution, and an example of a category that we had assumed reached its capacity and was then taken to the next level.

Often, the innovator who develops a successful strategy, campaign, or product enjoys a short-lived victory. If imitation is the sincerest form of flattery, then the **Octopus** marketer (See the chapter on SHARKS) compliments every innovative Brand A that is quickly followed to market by Brand B, Brand C, Brand D…

But as an award-winning marketer who has always strived to produce dynamic creative efforts on every single initiative, I would rather focus on what the leader does to become the buzz of the category rather than those who follow. And that brings us to Laird.

For those of you who are not familiar with surfing great Laird Hamilton, I will provide a little context so that we can properly learn how to create an original campaign from a man who rides waves bigger than the building you work in. Laird is to surfing as Charles Saatchi, Donny Deutsch, Bill Veeck, and Henry Ford are to marketing. A high school dropout, Laird has become the poster child for big wave surfing, is married to former model and pro volleyball star Gabrielle Reece, and has a thriving career in the surf industry across many platforms. Yet it is his constant innovation and creative thinking that has lead us to use him as *The Surfer's Guide To Marketing* symbol of creativity.

We all know creative people and they are more often than not an integral part of the marketing process. While a designer or copywriter can produce good creative and they may be some of the more creative resources available, this chapter is looking to explore every marketing professional's inner creative abilities. Not just the truly gifted creative types. By using the Hamilton example, you will see that even the most analytical thinking MBA-type can develop their creative perspective and apply simple *"what if's"* to solve problems, create new revenue streams, or develop an innovative marketing campaign.

This is by far my favorite subject because, as an extremely creative thinker, I often see things that others can't. Ideas pop up like visions, slogans appear instantly out of thin air, or the *"what if"* question rings loudly in my head non-stop twenty-four hours a day. Perhaps you are wired in a similar manner and thinking "outside the box" comes easy to you.

Like a singer with a naturally good voice, they can't explain how they have right tone, rhythm, actually hear or feel the music inside their head. It's an amazing and natural gift that as a 6'4" white guy who dances like a 6'8" white guy can't possibly fathom. I am fascinated by how musicians have rhythm or how someone can push down on piano keys and make it sound anything more than the dying cat noise I produce.

It's a gift, a talent, and a point of differentiation that I strongly believe should always be valued and maximized. Creative concepts and activations set themselves apart from the rest of the world. We should again emphasize that we are discussing the presentation of opportunities in a unique light to create potential or find new solutions, not just those who have an ability to draw. While some may have more creative abilities than others, let's look at Laird and his career as a shining example of utilizing good creativity to develop the future.

The title of this chapter is TOW-IN SURFING and the extreme sport serves as the signature creative feat on Hamilton's resume. While we will explore several of his contributions to the sport of surfing, the tow-in discovery is a great case study in terms of creating a new way of thinking by utilizing what everyone else also had access to but didn't think to develop.

Surfing has been around since the 1700's when Captain James Cook noted that Polynesian locals in the South Pacific rode "canoes" without paddles in the waves for fun. And Clayton Jacobsen in 1973 invented the personal watercraft (or more commonly known by its brand name, *Jet Ski®*). Yet for decades, no one thought of combining the two until Hamilton had his "peanut butter and chocolate" brainstorm in the early 1990's.

I can confidently say that I am strong at marketing, average (at best) at surfing, and not much of a physicist, so when I explain the basics of a big wave, it's simplistic at best. The largest waves in the world including Cortes Bank, Maverick's, Aileen's, Ghost Tree, etc. all are simply too large, too powerful, and too swift for a human to paddle into. If you paddle at five miles per hour and huge monster waves travel in extent of forty miles per hour… you can do the math. While noted exceptions like Greg Noll's epic day in 1969 where he had multiple legendary rides notwithstanding, even the most experienced and talented surfers simply couldn't catch the big giants. And so the surfing law was simply accepted that there are just some waves we will never conquer.

While countless surfers and millions more land-bound humans have stared into the sea, watched waves crash, and experienced various surfing conditions around the world, it was Hamilton and his surfing buddies Darrick Doerner and Buzzy Kerbox who changed the face of surfing only a few decades ago. They simply looked at an obvious solution; if the waves were faster than the surfers could paddle, let's speed up the surfers. They sought to find a way to incrementally add speed to the surfer and the list of solutions were so basic, yet plausible, that they were almost too obvious. After a few tweaks with rubber boats and personal water-crafts featuring water ski tow ropes attached, the big wave phenomenon had begun. It looks obvious now, but *you* didn't think of it!

I liken the tow-in case to disposable toilet brushes. Scrub brushes have been around for as long as we've had indoor plumbing yet it took some product developer (or maybe even a marketing mind) to realize a used brush that has just done the unthinkable in your toilet doesn't need to be put back under the sink. A simple tweak to add a disposable end, plastic button to eject the used portion without touching the dirty bristles, and a disposable brush you can throw away is born. So obvious. And so brilliant! But I will admit for this discussion, it's way cooler to invent a way to ride sixty-foot waves than to clean toilets.

TOW IN SURFING

SURF LESSON

GET CREATIVE

This is by far the hardest lesson to quantify because you can't just tell someone to "be creative". But better understanding how I approach an opportunity and allowing you to follow the steps and break down the process into smaller, obtainable snippets is the same approach a surf instructor takes when they have a student stand up on dozens of foot-high ankle slappers before having them put it all together on a larger wave. Look at the problem or situation, use your left-brained logic to think of what the end point or desired outcome would be, and then utilize your right-brain abstract thinking to brainstorm different ways to get from A to B.

Or more accurately, how to get from A to C using elements B as the creative solution. A + B = C.

A) QUESTION THE BRAND - The first

thing we do when we are challenged with a new marketing opportunity is to dissect what the brand has been through, what it stands for, and where it would like to go. Simply list the pros/cons of the current brand.

B) GOAL – Where are we today (Point A) and where do we ultimately want to be (Point C)? For this exercise, we will refer to our end point as C in order to add the elements to get there (referred to as B). Perhaps we were once an every-day sneaker but we want to enter the high performance category. Maybe we want to focus our all-natural food as a healthy line instead of the traditional meal that Mom used to make. Create a destination by listing the ideal positioning your brand would like to achieve and some of the key descriptive terms that you would ideally want your brand or product to be perceived as.

C) INVENTORY - What resources do you have access to? It's easy to say we want to drive impressions so having a website, we must then drive advertising. But looking at the website and your current advertising plan, break it down and see what parts you like and what you'd like to improve. Let the creative ideas flow by simply putting together a long list of all the "tools" you have to get to Point C.

D) FILL IN THE GAPS - Once the general map is established, start the brainstorming process to address smaller ways (or B) to get from A to C. Think of this as a math problem and rather than having to immediately solve $A = C$, lets come up with abstract ways to solve *to get to* C and have B = your creative solutions.

Now put it all together so $A + B = C$. (There may not be just one element to get you there so it could be $B + B2 + B3 + B4 + B5...$) These creative ideas can be broken down and ranked on plausibility and effectiveness for each step and then when put in conjunction with one another, you should start to flow to fill in the gaps. I often think that a blank slate is actually more difficult to create from because there are too many possibilities and being challenged with how to take Product A to level X may seem like a daunting task when looking at the whole of the challenge.

A more simple, obtainable form of creative thinking comes when you are faced with a problem, a set of variables, and a desired outcome. Trying to fill in the blanks between points working in reverse to get from here to there. It's easier than having to solve a gigantic proposition. Like the tow-in case where the question (how do I ride big waves?) was broken down to A (what do we do currently = paddle with our arms) and B (what resources do we have to go faster = personal water craft, tow rope, etc.) Without looking at all the options and stepping back from how we currently look at the problem, Laird's answer might have been to either simply try to paddle faster or give up. If he only thought about trying to use human

power to go faster, he might have
spent five hours a day trying to bulk
up to get stronger (not that *that* is
Hamilton's problem since the guy is
yoked!) but instead, he was able to
look at other elements to bring into the
equation that had not been part of the
board + guy + nothing else equation
that had been used to-date. Basically,
add in every imaginable element,
strategy, or abstract thought and
through elimination and tweaking,
discover the best path to get you to
the end result.

Hamilton has continued to serve as the shining
example of where surfers and marketers meet as he is
also responsible for what I in 2013, am calling the next
big sport/activity. Like windsurfing was in the 1980's
and snowboarding in the 2000's, I see Laird's stand up
paddleboard (SUP) as the next big outdoor activity.
While surfboards and paddles have been stored
together in sheds and beach houses for dozens of
years, it was our big wave icon that is credited with
developing an arm of the sport to satisfy surfers with a
new twist or a completely new activity when the exact

opposite of big waves are available. Utilizing a larger, thicker, wider board and a longer paddle, SUP paddleboards allow surfers to enjoy the ocean on flat days or any body of water to experience the good vibe of the outdoors while getting quite a workout in at the same time. And the SUP paddleboards can be seen from oceans, to bays, to surf spots, and are popping up everywhere including the rivers around New York City.

Creative thinking for marketing purposes is taking what we already have, what we know we'd like to do with it, and then creating an innovative way doing something unique to get the results. The *Jet Ski®* and the surfboard were always there, we just needed Laird to show us how they fit together.

On a side note, Hamilton and his friends also developed the first foot straps on the board (while trying to pull off the first 360°), which later became a staple of most big wave surfboards. While being able to create novel campaigns, products, or strategies may come easier for certain thinkers like Hamilton, it's not to say that we can't maximize our abilities and push the creative thinking beyond our normal levels.

I classify two types of marketing minds for simple reference; "creative marketers" and "spreadsheet marketers". Both have unique values and talents they bring to the table but tend to fall into the stereotypical left-brain or right-brain category. A creative marketer is Laird Hamilton. A man who sees opportunity and *"what if"* wherever he goes. I have been a creative thinker my entire life and while successful concepts pop into my head in an instant, I have always struggled with spreadsheet-type marketing roles. CPG brand marketers tend to look at P&L's more than packaging copy and use analytical talents and budget crunching skills far more often than their right-brained creative counterparts. Those in the creative group tend to more easily come up with the promotional elements, sweepstakes, or event themes.

Both are equally needed in the business world and while the more creative minds might be great at developing unique elements for a product or designing brand-new POP, they may not have the makeup to apply creative thinking to a schematic or finding incremental revenue in a budget. They say *"the devil is in the details"* and the left-brained spreadsheet marketers hold the advantage by generally being more micro-focused. Again, not applicable to every marketing or business person but I would wager that your more creative, outside-the-box thinkers probably need a little more effort in managing the small moving parts than a general direction.

I am definitely guilty of being a dynamic creative thinker who often has to work backwards to fill in the details. I have actually had to teach myself to double (and triple) check everything so that the "spreadsheet marketer" in me catches up to the creative marketing side. Otherwise when I'm multitasking (like trying to create amazing marketing efforts for clients while simultaneously writing a future best-selling book), I would miss details, have incomplete projects or thoughts and generally th

(Yes, that was a joke.) But you get the idea of my strengths and weaknesses and how they can both be utilized to create marketing success. Just like different types of surfers from soul surfing grandpas to soccer moms to twelve-year-old wall riders, different types of marketing minds can add value and complement each other and everyone can leverage creativity in their given roles.

In the Hamilton examples, we simple explore opportunities that may have been available for many other surfers yet one man made the difference. There may be a "standard price' for packaging cardboard or a set media buy that's worked well for years but that doesn't mean you should accept it or be content. Simply look at it from a different perspective, inject your *"what if"* creative approach and explore alternatives.

Having been fortunate enough to win many creative marketing awards, I am often asked how I come up with concepts that resonate so well with the targeted demographic. While there isn't a science to creative thinking, I have noted my usual personal creative development process and attempted to demonstrate how my talent works.   It always starts with the same question; *what would be the ultimate X for this brand?* If it's a sweepstakes, I think about what the product is, what it's users look for, and if I could do *anything* with the brand, what would that be?

When we worked with *ESPN* on their *Monday Night Football* promotion, an obvious prize is to meet a famous player. But what would be the *ultimate* version of that prize? As a football fan I'd love to actually spend time with a legend… at a game… and be able to hear inside knowledge from someone who has been there. And even better, how about doing that with *multiple* players! *That* is taking it to the next level. Take what a consumer might expect and then give them more. It exceeds their perception of what is good and takes it to the "great" level. (The final campaign had *four* Hall of Famers with iconic *Monday Night Football* moments in the suite with the winner).

When our client wanted to launch its business television network, they insisted on having a briefcase kit as their collateral. It was an idea that, while somewhat predictable, was pretty much the direction they were locked in on. Our concern was that unless executed well, it could be a very obvious and predictable medium for a business network and not garner much attention. After all, isn't a briefcase a little cliché?

Our mission was to bring "a little party" to the all-business impression that the kit currently represented.

We analyzed the materials and wondered how we could add some sizzle to the kit that also showcased the actual product. In this case, the 24-hour business network is promoting its on-air content, the channel itself. So how do we best sample a product that doesn't typically fit inside a briefcase like a tube of toothpaste or a new granola bar? If their "product" is television, then let's give them television!

We added a small video player, light-activated power source and a DVD of promotional spots and before we knew it, we had a marketing kit that had a "wow" factor of instant TV in a suitcase that actually demonstrated the product... the on-air highlights from the network.

I often say that the only thing cooler than winning a brand new 42" flat-screen TV in a sweepstakes is *not* winning a 42" flat-screen TV in a sweepstakes! I truly believe that if you have the ability to select an experience or once-in-a-lifetime reward that adds buzz and can't be bought at the local electronics store, you will get significantly more traction. When utilizing creative thought to make the exclusive reward a desirable and exciting prize that is still on-brand and communicates the benefits of the product or service, you can advance the campaign much in the same way Hamilton did with surfing.

Creating an innovative new project or enhancing the current version each require creativity and can produce the eye-catching results you seek if done well. The business network example shows that a simple addition makes for an amazing result and while some of you reading this might even think that adding a mini DVD player inside an actual briefcase to show a TV network in action isn't really that amazing, I would probably argue with you... if I wasn't too busy cleaning the shelf full of marketing trophies that it received.

TOW-IN SURFING

CASE STUDY

ONCE IN A LIFETIME EXPERIENCE

A well-known sports network approached us with an opportunity to provide VIP tours of their East Coast studios. They originally wanted to use them as a VIP or advertising incentive (which they had done numerous times in the past) and had not really thought of much more in terms of leveraging this unique prize. And frankly, aside from the studio itself, the surrounding area doesn't particularly have the vacation destination appeal of Hawaii or Tahiti or Belize.

So, we quickly looked at what we had in terms of access to the hallowed grounds that all sports fans are familiar with and decided that we could create a really unique, buzz-worthy promotion that would bring the network significantly more marketing return than what they saw at the time and create significantly more participation from fans.

By developing a weekend prize experience that mirrored the famous network commercials, we could allow fans to live the unique elements and make a trip to the studio seem like winning the lottery! As the network's sports anchor would announce in the on-air spot, VIPs/ contest winners would experience *"athletes at the water cooler and mascots running the cameras"* just like the legendary ad campaign implied.

From the time winners arrived in the small airport and were greeted by an NCAA cheer squad and mascot, to being checked into the hotel by the iconic Hall of Famer Rollie Fingers (he of the large handle-bar mustache), to the tour and lunch in the famous cafeteria, and finally arriving in New York for a Yankees game and having dinner at a famous sports-themed restaurant with head chef William "The Refrigerator" Perry, we took an existing asset (a studio tour) and created a desirable campaign around it that exceeded the network's expectations.

All by taking what we had access to and creating a greater story and experience around the basic elements. It was mostly adding "window dressing" but it still created a desirable experience instead of a ho-hum promotion and communicating it in a much bigger fashion. It's simply a process of looking at what you have, where you want to be, and how can you present or add components that make your lemons into lemonade.

A logical direction for this chapter is to continue to explore those who have proven that creative thinking, need-based solutions, and the perennial *"what if?"* mantra. I have worked with some of the most creative minds in the world of marketing and one of my favorite people to learn from and observe is one of the true pioneers in sports television, Mr. David Hill. For those of you not familiar with Mr. Hill and his legendary accomplishments in the way we view television, here is a brief rundown of some of his greatest innovations:

Want to see the score of your game, time left, and other details? Thank David for creating the "Fox Box" that has all of the game's stats on screen throughout the contest. Hard time following the puck on TV during NHL games... watch David's glowing puck. Catcher Cam. Diamond Cam. You get the point

Bringing the NFL to *Fox* in 1993 seemed like an impossible task but working for Rupert Murdoch, that's precisely what David was able to do. Along with incredible vision and having his finger on the pulse of what viewers want, Hill was able to constantly provide noteworthy innovations that have all but become commonplace in today's world. In fact, try to find a sporting event on television that *doesn't* have a signature Hill enhancement (NASCAR's *Digger the Gopher* Cam not withstanding).

While working at *Fox*, I had the pleasure on occasion to

learn from David Hill and there are few people in the world I respect more for both his passion, creativity, and caviler attitude. If you speak with David, the congenial Australian, you would never guess that he is an icon in the sports broadcasting world and responsible for so many amazing innovations. He's funny, gregarious, humble, and once gave me a three-word sentence praising a project of mine that started with *"That's"* ended with *"awesome"* and had an F-bomb in the middle! He's my hero.

I sought out the opportunity to sit down with David for this chapter as no conversation about creative thinking and innovative philosophies would be as good without the legendary exec's input. And maybe because he spent his youth *"playing hooky in Australia to go surfing instead of learning"* as he mentioned to me, he was kind enough to spend a few minutes with me at his office on the studio lot.

The frank answer David gave me when addressing the secret to creative thinking was simple; discover what *isn't* there and build it. He observed that many of his incredible innovations came from his perception of what was missing. A creative thinker visualizes the end product and David is no different. The mind works either logically or laterally and a right-brained thinker tends to work with the latter. Just like in the SURF

LESSON for this chapter, see where you want to go (what's missing) and work backwards to fill in the gaps. David sees the end or results and then works in reverse to address the details or components that get to the ultimate goal.

As he pointed out to me, most of the significant inventions of the modern generation occurred between 1880 and 1910. The light bulb, radio, television, automobile, etc. all were derived in a short timeframe where inventors began to find glaring needs that would incrementally advance our culture.

Philo Farnsworth, the father of television, came up with the concept of transmitting pictures in "waves" or "rows" by staring at a plowed corn field as a teen. He had always wanted to find a way to transmit pictures (and eventually video) and knew what his end results looked like. While working hard on the farm, he found the solution to the vision by seeing the equal rows of crops and how you could transmit lines of images separately versus the whole thing at once and thus, as his B solution, he was able to get from A to C by plowing ahead.

David was able to run through the origins of his greatest accomplishments and they all address a need to fix what we are missing. After spending some time with Mr. Hill and hearing his tales of innovation, I can honestly say that if necessity is the mother of invention, then David Hill is one creative mother!

TOW-IN SURFING

CASE STUDY

THINK *INSIDE THE BOX*

As a long-time television executive, David Hill had been around the world and had seen virtually every top network's broadcasts from cricket to baseball to sailing. And one night, while having a pint and watching a European soccer (football) match in his favorite pub, he hit on what would become his signature innovation.

The game, which Hill described as "boring" featured uninterested, "lazy" announcers who droned on and on. He said he was bored to tears and had been watching for over twenty minutes when it occurred to him that he didn't know the score, how much time was left, etc. The announcers' babble didn't include any of the facts he was seeking.

He had an "A-ha" moment (not the band from the 80's) where he realized he should add a scoreboard on screen. It was brilliant, simple, obvious... and *hated* at first!

Death threats from sports "purists" aside, David created the "new" element that was quickly dubbed the "Fox Box". (Hill says he wished it had been named the *Hill* Box as his standing legacy). This innovation is a staple on every broadcast today but up until David noticed a need to accent the lackluster broadcasters' mediocre performance that day, no one had vision to think *inside* the box during telecasts!

If we learn anything from surfing huge waves that a decade ago were deemed too big and too dangerous, let it be that tow-in surfing and aquatic pioneer Laird Hamilton risked his life because he believed that through his creativity and innovation, he could advance his sport. So think of what you perceive as standard process, what your brand currently communicates, what resources you typically use, or what the category stands for today and challenge it. I promise that even if you don't create the next big sport or automobile or sportscasting component, your risk will never be as great as being crushed by a 40-foot wave. Or touching a dirty toilet brush.

"Surfing is climbing from a warm bed in pre-dawn's coolness a sleepy drive, coffee and doughnuts at a roadside diner and the clatter of surfboards as they're unstacked from the car rack. Surfing is the joy of watching a sunrise slowly into the sky. It's crisp, clean waves, crests blown high by an offshore wind. It's gray mist, dampness and cold sand under bare feet, the lonely cry of a gull sweeping across silent, brooding seas."

–Fred Wardy

CHAPTER 5

LIFESTYLE

Live your brand. It makes life so much more fulfilling if the 50-60 hours you spend marketing your brand per week at least reaches some emotional cord inside you that provides incremental satisfaction. Speaking the language, understanding the product, and being part of the target in some form or fashion makes life a whole lot easier than trying to force it as an outsider.

The surfing world is made up of former hard core surfers or weekend warriors who truly enjoy their hobby beyond the two to three hours they are actually in the water. They tend to live the *Lifestyle*, breathe the culture, support the brands, and associate with like-minded consumers. In essence, living among the gorillas in the rain forest allows you to think, process, and live like a gorilla.

Living at the beach and wearing flip-flops 24/7 are not the only *Lifestyle* requirements of a surfer. But just by the nature of the mind-set, culture, ambiance, and attitude of where I live and who I associate with allows me to better align with the *Lifestyle* than say a Minnesota teen whose only exposure to the surf brand is in their local mall. It goes without saying that the more the marketer eats, sleeps, and lives their brand or demographic, the more familiar they will become with it. Creating the right tone, message, and benefits would come much easier if you spoke the right language.

There are dozens of classic examples of companies that communicate a message that worked well in one culture and then trying to carry it on to a different community with disastrous results. It's not that the actual text or translation was incorrect, but not understanding the culture's language or nuances can make the converted campaign a little less than desirable in the new application. *Coors* beer once had a *"Turn It Loose,"* campaign, and when converted to Spanish, was *"Suffer From Diarrhea."* Pepsi's *"Come Alive With the Pepsi Generation"* lost something in the translation when it informed the Chinese demographic that *"Pepsi Brings Your Ancestors Back From the Grave."* So when *"It won't leak in your pocket and embarrass you"* seemed like a good concept for a pen company, the misuse of the word "embarazar" in Spanish told our friendly neighbors to the South that their product *"won't leak in your pocket and make you pregnant."*

While these are extreme examples of how a casual lack of understanding of the culture, language or **Lifestyle** can cause great embarrassment, it's not uncommon for your marketing efforts to suffer if the demo feels it's being sold to. If your company targets sensitive demographics, they need to be even more carefully approached with the campaign to ensure it's organic. Fish that are prey tend to be much more skittish than a large, gliding predator who slowly moves along in the open. Going after the general male demo is a much more straightforward approach than a segmented female 'tween group that is subject to fickle opinions and sensitive to trends.

Believe me that understanding the culture is a way to

save time and embarrassment.   As an America backpacker in Europe who once approached a group of British females and announced that *"I am Randy"*, (in essence announcing that *"I am horny"*) I understand that living the **Lifestyle** is key to communicating your brand accurately.

When we cast Brand Ambassadors for the various tours, events, and projects, we go beyond finding models or actresses that simply look good. We want to ensure they truly represent the brand and align favorably with the demographic they are targeting. The most common denominator we have is an attractive female model that doesn't cause a 45-year-old man to run away when they approach. Add their experience coaxing information from the consumer or presenting the brand in a positive manor and we have a much more productive engagement. Yes, it goes without saying that a pretty girl can give out a product sample, coupon, or message much more successfully than your average unshaven, overweight man in a half-shirt. They say *"sex sells"* and while I don't take it to that extent, an attractive, intelligent, friendly Brand Ambassador can do wonders with an uninterested consumer.

But beyond the general masses, we have found that Hispanic models that can speak the language fluently will have a much greater impact communicating our Spanish language client's product than their English-only peer. It makes sense on the surface but it goes beyond the simple language barrier. Consumers like to associate with brands or those representatives who serve as a seamless extension of the brand and assimilate to the consumer.   A younger Brand Ambassador at a rock concert can engage teens better than a more "sophisticated adult" nine out of ten times. And women at the mall are easily engaged in a product sample if the hired staff appears to be in their similar situation and could possibly be seen shopping right alongside them if they were not working the booth itself.

It may sound obvious but too often companies forget the details when plotting out their marketing campaigns and never realize that those little subtle details can sabotage the entire effort. They will hire the first ten people who apply at a lesser rate rather than doing a little more work and casting a team that accurately and positively represents the brand and the demographic. In the world of price over value, marketing companies seem to be more content with ten inexpensive, less professional, *Craigslist* hires that cannot communicate fluently over five professional Brand Ambassadors who, beyond their physical attributes, have the experience and personalities to be significantly more effective. If these people are an extension of your brand and you opt for non-congruent, "average" people who just want to pass out fliers for minimum wage, then what are you saying about your product?

We did a pro football campaign where our Street Team's objective was to drive interest and demand for a league-branded product. Along with the requirements of youthful, experienced, intelligent, and attractive Brand Ambassadors, we ensured that the team we hired were all fans of the local pro football teams in the various markets. While it sounds like a small qualifier since the average interaction between the consumer and our Brand Ambassadors was mere minutes, it made a huge difference. When our team approached a group of jersey-wearing Giants fans in a New York pub, along with the product message and key talking points, they were able to chat up the news of the day, the team's recent win, and whether Michael Strahan was better than Lawrence Taylor. The team lived that *Lifestyle*, was able to create a deeper bond. And due to their instant ties with the fans, they could create stronger influence and ultimately have a higher percentage of their consumers achieve a positive call-to-action. All things considered, wouldn't you want someone who uses the brand to promote the brand?

LIFESTYLE

CASE STUDY

SKATE, SURF, SNOW

When we launched an action sports network, featuring skateboarding, surfing, Moto-X, snowboarding, and more, we created many on-site events that promoted the network among teens and 'tweens. We did skate park demos with Wee Man and Ryan Sheckler and had significant amounts of giveaways and branding. As the point person for the brand, I was there on-site to ensure everything went well and communicate with the consumers in what I thought would be successful impromptu focus groups. What I discovered quickly was that thousands of savvy kids thought that the big guy in the tie must be a narc of some sort and treated me with the same respect as a shark in a guppy tank. Cold!

While I may think I am a soul surfer and a card-carrying member of the action sports tribe, my *Lifestyle* as a surfer doesn't translate directly to the hard-core ten-year-old skate set. I understand their passion for this **Lifestyle** and more than some people my age I think I can relate to an extent. But the lingo, the attitude, and the true skate culture is lost on me. And heaven forbid I drop a *"radical"*, *"tubular"*, or *"gnarly"* reference in an attempt to act cool and assimilate which would ultimately serve to alienate myself further. You don't always have to *be* the demographic to market to the demographic. I'm simply stating that being well-versed and passionate about the brand or the demo makes it easier to communicate and probably more interesting. Regardless of whether you live the **Lifestyle**, you need to be fluent in the world or else be called out as a narc!

I use the analogy that a cardiologist doesn't need to have had a heart attack to understand the situation and how much a disgruntled ticker can hurt. Likewise, I can market to twenty-five-year-old females without having been one (minus one bad Halloween, but we won't go there). Regardless of the demo, you have to at least *appear* authentic and credible to communicate accurately and seamlessly, lest you want to stand out like a grown-up freak among long-haired skater kids!

They tell writers to *"write what you know"* and that is a good mantra to live by in the spirit of the LIFESTYLE chapter. I produced this book on marketing tips and secrets because if I was challenged to create a literary work on physics, it would be a very short pamphlet. But having been in the trenches and having observed and learned successful tricks of the trade from people who are way smarter than I was, I have lived, breathed, and experienced countless marketing efforts. It's in my DNA and it's part of my **Lifestyle**. Add to that the niche I have chosen in the sports and entertainment space and I am maximizing all of my hot buttons on a daily basis. With ever evolving opportunities, you need to be fluent in traditional marketing so you can focus on understanding and maximizing emerging trends and if you are playing catch-up and not immersed in the **Lifestyle**, you won't be able to keep up with the new opportunities.

Using my previous example of writing what you know,

had this been *The Farmers Guide To Marketing*, it would be a challenging task for me to produce a book as I'm not too knowledgeable or interested in harvesting anything. Hell, it's hard enough to draw hundreds of surf and oceanic references for this book when I do know about that, so imagine how bad the puns would be if this was set against farming. I'd be beet!

LIFESTYLE

SURF LESSON

I LOVE YOU

As I mentioned in the start of the book, part of the mission of *The Surfers Guide To Marketing* is to motivate you to excel in your career. Aside from the theories, samples, and suggestions we discuss in this future standard college marketing curriculum textbook, I want to challenge you to do what makes you the most successful marketer you can be! Having been on both sides of the fence promoting both products I enjoy and also brands I have no interest in, I can definitely conclude that if all things are equal, engaging in something you are passionate about gives you a distinct advantage.

This chapter's SURF LESSON is to challenge you to look at your current status and map out your future. While you may be content doing what you do or may be incredibly successful doing something you don't enjoy, life is too short to not leave your mark in the places you want to. Any old-time surfer will tell you that the experience of a surf session is greater than just the act of surfing. The zen, the emotions, the *Lifestyle*. It's the subjective aspect of the activity more than just the activity itself. It's rare that a famous football player dislikes the competition of a game or an academic professor dislikes helping her students learn and grow. And let's face the facts; if you are stuck in a cubicle or office ten to twelve hours a day discussing work, it might as well be something that stokes your fire.

A) WHO ARE YOU? – Take a moment

and list your favorite interests, hobbies, and brands. While everyone loves *their* children, you may not love *all* children so try to list things that go beyond basics like your immediate family. Write down your favorite forms of entertainment, activities, interests, and the products you enjoy or find valuable in your life. Listing your top sports or television networks may be easy but don't limit yourself to just those genres.

Think of yourself as a famous athlete and every company wants you to endorse their product. What company or brand would love to have your name associated with it? Do you use a certain seasoning on your secret cooking recipe and swear by it? Do you tell all of your friends about your smart phone and why they should switch? If you were able to invest your hard-earned pesos in one brand you believe in, what would you put your name on the line for? No matter how far-fetched, write down all of the brands or industries you would love to bring your talents to.

B) PRIORITIZE – Take a look at the items on your list and rank them based on a combination of interest, feasibility, and possibility.

1) Interest – if you are a huge wine connoisseur and are very knowledgeable about the different varietals for example, that might rank ahead of your casual watching of weekend NCAA basketball games.

2) Feasibility – If you enjoy space ships you still may not be able to go into the NASA marketing program as a realistic career based on the limited need for space shuttle marketing.

3) Possibility – Does the interest or interests have solid career opportunities? If your passion for fashion provides hundreds to even thousands of realistic jobs or career paths has more of a realistic possibility than your other passion of snorkeling, then maybe that becomes the highest ranking item on your list.

C) TEST THE WATER- Now that you have your list in order of your favorite interests combined with the most realistic opportunities, see how warm the ocean is. Stick a toe in. With the internet and great sites like *LinkedIn* or *Glassdoor*, you can quickly research various companies, fields, etc. And if you are looking to create a career in a **Lifestyle** that you are already engaged in off-the-clock, then you should be very familiar with the top companies, brands, and players. Put out some feelers or see who you know who is connected in the space you want to be in.

D) DROP IN – Any surfer will tell you that dropping in on a wave is a risky move. You may pull it off, you may wipe out, or you may make some enemies of guys you cut off. Exploring a new industry can be just as trying but if you work at it, you might just pull off a great ride!

Perhaps you can volunteer for a group that works in your ideal industry or maybe can spend nights/weekends doing something that entrenches you in the **Lifestyle** your hobby entails. Basically find ways to get relevant experience for that particular interest.

Blogging is another "internship" you might utilize to gain experience in an industry. Start a blog that allows you to become engaged in the industry you would like to be in and showcase your opinion, creativity, knowledge, etc. ESPN is full of bloggers who contribute now. There are countless fashion sites where "amateurs" post their OOTD (*Outfit Of The Day* for you non-hip readers) that allow the writers to gain access to the industry, make contacts, and even earn product to review.

When people tell me they want to work in sports and want me to hire them because they can name every member of the Dallas Cowboys, I tell them they are a fan. If a person tells me they interned for the team, wrote a thesis on better solutions to socially connect the team with the fans, or spends weekends as an equipment manager's assistant just to learn about the team from the logistical side, I am more than impressed.

While it helps if your dad owns a team or your mother was an executive at your favorite beverage company, no one is keeping you from gaining entry into the company that fits your *Lifestyle* but you!

Odds are if you are reading this book, you are a more junior professional or marketing novice. This message is aimed directly at you versus the fifty-year-old with kids and a large mortgage but it's applicable to everyone; life is short, be proud of what you do, and find something that allows your passion to come out and I guarantee you will think of your career as less of a job and more of an exciting challenge!

While there has to be generalizations when writing a

book to the masses, usually you will find that those who engage with a passion-based brand or industry in their personal life have a lifetime of experience or a track record of success in a similar field professionally.

Now, please don't assume that only 260lb. men who run a 4.4 forty-yard dash can market *Under Armour*, but it doesn't hurt to have an extended familiarity with the brand. You live the **Lifestyle**, you communicate the brand. Your relationship with your brand needs to be authentic so you can communicate the message authentically.

Taking *Under Armour* as an example; the well-documented story about CEO Kevin Plank as a former NCAA athlete playing football at the University of Maryland who found a need in the sport (performance shirts to go under shoulder pads). Because he was a player, he did set the tone for the brand and give it a form of credibility. The *"by the user, for the user"* story is a powerful one and filled a need. Just as Sara Blakely did when she invented *SPANX* to create a slimming garment for women and instantly answered the "why" for consumers. Even if you are not a true user of the product you market, you should ensure that those who engage the consumer at the one-to-one level are positioned to be the ideal demographic. Otherwise, you look like a big goofy narc walking among teens.

I once worked for a dog food company and it was indeed that… work. Every day was a tiring, boring chore. I was miserable and struggling to get by even though the job's skill set and talent requirement were the same set I had excelled with in previous roles. One of my coworkers, a dog breeder and enthusiast, was doing amazing work while putting in about half the effort that I seemed to be doing. Her results were always the best on the team and I studied her behavior, skill set, technique, and effort. I emulated her and tried to mirror her style, pitch, and creative campaigns and yet I fell farther behind in the (dog) race to succeed.

It soon became apparent that when I walked into a client's office or even their retail pet store (with a person who based his/her livelihood on the pet food industry), I showed up as only half-engaged based on ignorance, lack of experience, and frankly lack of passion. It wasn't intentional but I just wasn't a good enough actor to constantly fake my enthusiasm for the pet industry so I might as well have been Michael Vick trying to market dog food! You can be knowledgeable (I wasn't), passionate (I wasn't) or even simply a consumer of the brand (I wasn't) and be able to bring *something* to the industry beyond the collateral, pricing, and rhetoric you are simply regurgitating. I was going through the motions but not bringing any spice to the meal. I guess you could say my marketing had no bite.

It was at this point in my dog food career, during a three-day seminar featuring slides of dog nutrition... and images of the results (re: dog poop) that I realized I would only excel in an industry that evoked my passion and a **Lifestyle** I could engage in. That may be just in my case but I think it definitely holds true on some level with most of us.

I have several fraternity brothers from college who have made a wonderful career selling carpet and flooring. I am very proud of their success and appreciate their efforts, results, and the nice life they are able to afford. While I'm not saying every person in the carpet company's marketing department goes home and rolls around on swatches of shag like it's made of money or spends Friday night looking at new fiber samples, the average marketing mind will excel in their position if they enjoy their product, truly believe in what they sell, or even use it beyond the standard service their product provides.

And remember, creating a product or brand isn't the only element that the **Lifestyle** effects. The way you communicate the brand, the packaging, the creative, all should reflect the **Lifestyle**. A product that is a real industry advancement may not necessarily lead to success if the "window dressing" doesn't match. A great example of how a simple tweak that better aligns with the demographic audiences' *Lifestyle* was told to me by oceanic pioneer and Body Glove co-founder, Bob Meistrell.

Bob and his brother Bill created *Body Glove* 60 years ago and incorporated their love of diving and ocean to create the world's first "athletic" wetsuit that wasn't a cumbersome commercial diver's suit. Up until they created the neoprene version, wetsuits were basically only for professional use and not much good to those in the growing 50's surf culture. Those huge diving suits that commercial divers wore could never be duplicated for the casual market and you wouldn't want to try to stand up on a surf board with those bulky drysuits. After WWII, there was a gap in the available diving equipment and it wasn't until the brothers developed their suit that the industry began to take off.

But even though they had a great product they knew, as members of the beach *Lifestyle*, would keep them warm and allow for movement, the suits sat on their *Dive 'N Surf* retail store shelves. I am fortunate to know Bob and I never mind listening to his stories about the history of the surf and dive culture and along with being his neighbor at the beach, I have the honor of relaying the moment when **Lifestyle** interjected into his brand.

LIFESTYLE

CASE STUDY

A GLOVE BY ANY OTHER NAME

Bill and Bob Meistrell actually had grown up in the midwest and made their way out to Southern California when they were young. Both fell in love with the ocean and the two brothers quickly entrenched themselves in the So Cal beach culture.

Working out of their *Dive 'N Surf* retail store, the boys had made many significant advancements in surfing and diving in the 50's and 60's and their latest invention, a neoprene wetsuit, was a wonderful product that was slow to take off. They knew the product was a great alternative to the bulky diving suits of the day and the added stretch and flexibility would surely be a hit with surfers and water enthusiasts. If only customers would buy it.

But they were not doing as well with the sales as they would have liked with their *"The Dive 'N Surf's Thermocline Wetsuit"*. The product was good but for whatever reasons they couldn't identify, sales didn't reflect it. So when the brothers brought in Duke Boyd, a marketing expert, entrepreneur and founder of the *Hang Ten* surf brand, they set about tweaking the "packaging" instead of the product. Bill and Duke got together one night and Boyd told him simply, *"You've got to rename the wetsuit. 'The Dive 'N Surf Thermocline Wetsuit' is a terrible name."*

The brothers who had already created oceanic innovations that succeeded, were confused—In their opinion, *"The Dive 'N Surf Thermocline Wetsuit"* accurately described what the product was, who made it, and where to find it.

Boyd felt the name wasn't helping and was "too technical" for the growing surf culture. Boyd bluntly asked, *"What makes your wetsuit different from anybody else's?"* The Meistrell brothers thought for a moment and one of them replied, *"Well, it fits like a glove."* Bingo!

Within hours of that conversation, Duke Boyd paid a graphic designer around $30 to create the now iconic "hand logo" that the company still incorporates today. *"That's a pretty good deal for an icon that's all over the world,"* Bob told me with a chuckle. The new *Body Glove* brand and logo instantly told a story and described what the product does to those living the **Lifestyle**.

Today, with sales in excess of $200M annually, surfers agree. The wetsuit is tailored to the **Lifestyle** of the surfer and the founders find that bringing their passion to their work fits them... *like a glove.*

Some industries, products, or services may not lend themselves the ability to bring extensive passion to the day job but more often than not, if you put a list of your hobbies, interests, and favorite brands, you could probably find positions within those organizations that makes your job more of a **Lifestyle**. Or some angle within the goods/services or platform resonates with you and stokes that fire. It could be the satisfaction of producing something that is superior in the industry, helps people beyond their expected level of service, or fills some emotional need that contributes to the overwhelming satisfaction of the job. Whatever it is that nurtures a spark beyond simply a paycheck will create incremental results in your performance.

While working as a product developer for a large company in Chicago, I was teamed with a dynamic, creative group that oversaw all of the licensed product development for the organization. We had virtually all of the sports licenses (my area of expertise) including NBA, NFL, MLB, and NASCAR, theatrical brands like Disney and Warner Bros., children's licenses, etc. My very eclectic peer was an absolute artist when it came to creating new concepts for *Gone With The Wind* or *The Wizard of Oz* while I often struggled to keep pace. (It probably would have helped if I had ever actually watched the movie since I thought his suggestion to create something with flying monkeys was not, in fact, a joke... To which I was the only one in the executive meeting who laughed out loud at the actual mention of flying monkeys!) Conversely, I would rattle off great concepts for a Michael Jordan or Brett Favre campaign while he would refer to the iconic #23 as the number on his *outfit*. It's all about familiarity, passion, and being immersed in the **Lifestyle** of the brand.

Being familiar with the culture, demographic, or industry in your personal life will pay dividends in your professional life. Understanding the motivations of your consumer because you relate personally will allow you to see the opportunity from their perspective. Knowing how to position it, what the response will be, and how the **Lifestyle** hot buttons can drive your revenue is a distinct advantage. Sometimes you don't know, you feel and that's generated by familiarity. When you understand your market, love your product, and grasp how to market the brand, you will love your life... style.

I sometimes sum up the **Lifestyle** dynamic with the quote from that old *Hair Club For Men* commercial where the guys says, *"I'm not just the owner, I'm also a client"*. If you are willing to put your head on the line (literally) then that seems like a pretty good endorsement for living that **Lifestyle**, right?

For another great CASE STUDY on a company owner who truly enjoys his product, let's look at the "fishy" success of Wing Lam, the founder of *Wahoo's Fish*

Tacos. Wing might as well be the mascot for the brand because his attitude, persona, and passion for the business would make an ideal character for his company.

LIFESTYLE

CASE STUDY

TASTY WAVES

The story of *Wahoo's Fish Tacos* is the perfect example of what it means to live a brand. Wing Lam and his two brothers, Ed and Mingo, were raised in the Southern California surf culture and would often gorge on delicious fish tacos while on surf trips to Mexico.

Eventually, they decided to import the fish taco to Orange County (California) and give it a unique twist. Taking what they knew from their lifestyle, they combined the fish taco with their Brazilian favorites and Asian inspired items. From grilling on the beach until they opened up their first official location, they always stayed true to something they appreciated as businessmen *and* surfers. The brothers decorated the original restaurant with the donations of near-by surf companies and that's how *Wahoo's Fish Taco* was born.

Wing describes how a young grom would go to the beach and if he ate one of their tacos on a summer day, they would forever associate the great taste with the positive emotions of a great surf session. Hence, it became part of that kid's lifestyle.

Because they were ingrained in the culture (and maybe because the food was just really good) *Wahoo's* quickly developed a loyal and steady following, to where some locals came in daily and servers automatically knew what their customer would order. They were more than a brand or a meal, they were fellow members of the community, the culture... the ***Lifestyle.***

To this day, Wing can still be found on-site at many community events and loving the lifestyle, customers, and the product they produce enables him to maintain a high level of excitement. During the course of our discussion on marketing practices and how *Wahoo's* got to where they are, Wing said something that resonated as the ideal quote to encapsulate this chapter on **Lifestyle**; I asked him who drives the *Wahoo's* truck at these surf events and runs the grill on the beach. He appeared surprised that I was even asking as he responded, *"I do. Why wouldn't I?"*

Love what you do. Live the **Lifestyle** you market. Why *wouldn't* you? Aloha, Wing!

"I think when a surfer becomes a surfer, it's almost like an obligation to be an environmentalist at the same time"

- Kelly Slater

CHAPTER 6

ENVIRONMENTALISTS

I would hate to be the one to label *Environmentalists* as selfish, but in essence, they are.   You may think I'm crazy (frankly, I'm surprised it took you six chapters to reach that conclusion) but no matter how noble of heart or pure of intentions, people tend to support causes that relate to or benefit themselves. It makes sense that those who champion an effort have a vested interest in the cause and this underlying theme is the basis for sound cause marketing.

The *Surfrider Foundation* is probably the best-known philanthropic organization in the surf world. The non-profit grassroots group is dedicated to the protection and enjoyment of the world's oceans, waves and beaches. Founded in 1984 by a handful of visionary surfers in Malibu, California, the *Surfrider Foundation* now maintains over 50,000 members and 90 chapters worldwide.

While no one would admit it's a good idea to throw his or her trash in the ocean, hurt a dolphin, or pollute their beach, it happens every day. So it's all of the **Environmentalists** who make up the *Surfrider Foundation* that are a great example of how you can use ethos, charity, and good-will to get your message across. As a supporter of the cause, I have even chosen to provide a portion of the proceeds of *"The Surfer's Guide To Marketing"* to surf-based charities.

One of the great surfing stereotypes is the hippie, earthy, "gnarly-dude" persona. While some surfers might be mistaken for Jeff Spicoli of the 80's hit *Fast Times At Ridgemont High*, the majority of wave riding enthusiasts are more like the average American who simply enjoys their hobby. (With the exception that most of them have a soft spot for the preservation of their playground; the ocean.) Even the casual surfer tends to index higher on environmental and ocean conservation that the average citizen which should be a surprise to exactly no one. Simply put, if you engage in something, you tend to have its best interest at heart and are more aware of that cause as it directly impacts you.

I would venture to guess that more people in Hawaii are prone to support causes that affect the wildlife of their islands than say, the giant panda. While the WWF (*World Wildlife Fund*, not the former group of guys who jump off the top ropes of the ring in *Speedos*) has millions of supporters and does admirable work, I believe that someone with a cancer-stricken family member or a Rocky Mountain hiking enthusiast is more likely to associate with charities that fight the disease or preserve the mountain trails than those who don't interact with the big black and white bears or live in China or Brooklyn or wherever pandas live.

While people say my surfing ability is garbage, at least I don't have to surf *in* garbage. I have participated in beach clean-ups and recycling programs and I'm not even a huge Green Planet-type of guy. Just a surfer that wants to have a nice place to paddle around in. So with millions of Americans having some passion, hobby, or interest that they would devote philanthropic interest towards, it makes this chapter on **Environmentalists** a relevant discussion on utilizing Non-profit or Cause Marketing to advance your brand.

Some people quickly become "offended" or perceive the use of charity to promote Corporate America as dirty, underhanded, or just plain unethical. Hell, I have had many discussions with people who believe that all cause efforts must be organic, developed exclusively for the purpose of good, and can have no ulterior motives. And I concur... *to a point.*

Before we get too much farther into the discussion, I want to be very clear that I firmly believe that Cause Marketing or charity involvement by a company's goods or services must include two key variables:

A) The charity is true, real, and genuinely benefits from the effort. There are examples of big corporations "creating" philanthropy or instituting a good will effort only to have the thinly veiled excuse for marketing backfire. If you want to devote resources, time, effort, dollars, etc. to a cause, then you must truly believe in the cause.

B) Developing a cause campaign or aligning with

an existing charity must be a natural partnership that is organic in nature and forms a positive, logical combination for the brand.

When you see Corporate America putting on their best front and showing the world how generous or caring they are, there can't be any red flags that question authenticity. A clothing company supporting *MADD (Mothers Against Drunk Driving),* while honorable and helping a great cause, still might seem lost in translation as a consumer might then question why their jeans are against drunk drivers. Again, a great cause or philanthropy but perhaps not organic to that particular brand. In other words, make sure the cause you engage in has direct relevance to what your brand stands for.

There are several different levels that could be used to form a symbiotic relationship in the realm of **Environmentalists** including the relevance of your brand, your company/industry proximity to the chosen cause or even a personal story that ties the brand to the philanthropy. Perhaps the previous blue jeans example isn't such a stretch if the founder of the company lost a loved one to a drunk driver in an accident. Or perhaps the CMO has a story about adversity that has challenged her to give back and champion the cause.

Great stories that bring a human side to the effort and a green-light for that brand to integrate in the fight in the eyes of their consumers is as good and authentic as it gets. Just so long as it's clear why the marketer is involving their brand. To the average consumer, not knowing the back story or the reason why a company is supporting a philanthropy isn't helping gain the marketing advantage. The users need to understand the motivation and relevance behind the cause or else it just falls flat from a marketing perspective (although hopefully *still* supporting a cause which is always good from the human perspective!)

The most common variable of a successful use of philanthropy in terms of marketing results is the relevance to the brand or the industry. The more congruent, the better. *SPEED Channel* which is a network for all-things automotive, makes a great partner for drinking and driving PSAs (Public Service Announcements). They show fellow auto enthusiasts that no matter how much you are involved with your vehicle, when it comes to drinking, don't get behind the wheel! Their talent and messaging is aligned to discuss a cause marketing effort surrounding vehicles.

General Mills marketing to kids and their parents,

does a great job with *Box Tops For Education* where proof of purchase collection directly dictates which local schools receive the benefits. The effort makes sense to an extent and the brand is spot-on in terms of "understanding" or relating to the key charity demographic and the cause. We all know the cereal industry thrives on getting kids "nutritional" starts to their day so they can go to school and learn so why not take it further and be a good partner *in* their classroom as well. Don't end at the breakfast table if you can get involved in the classroom and expose your brand even more.

But just because you are speaking to the right audience with the right brand doesn't mean you are building a positive philanthropic effort. It's an obvious effort to sell more cereal because the more box tops means more dollars for *your* school... which means more sales for *GM*. It does work because parents want to help their kids and local schools and since they have to eat anyway... why not feed them more of *GM*'s products, right?

It makes sense to have a kid's cereal talk about scholastic efforts when they don't really get in the way of education. In fact, I've never heard a child say he's torn between reading a book and reading a cereal box so I guess they are immune to most negative connotations with that particular cause. But what if your brand or product *isn't* a neutral party just trying to help?

Beer companies spend hundreds of millions to fight drunk driving. Cigarette manufacturers spend countless hours trying to discourage minors from purchasing or using their products. And all of that cause marketing is a flimsy attempt to look good when in fact they are responsible for the negative issue in the first place. (Ok, so I don't get sued, let's say they *might* be partially responsible for these issues). Are you really doing a good deed when you are half of the problem in the first place?

Take the tragedy in the Gulf and *British Petroleum* or *BP*. While they don't forever want to be the bad guys who practically destroyed an entire ecosystem, their little PR spin and commercials about how much they are spending and giving back to the Gulf Coast is a little insulting. Of course you should be doing the right thing; *you caused the problem!!!* That is less about being **Environmentalists** who are trying to use goodwill to drive their brand as it is a PR attempt to not be perceived as bad guys. It follows along the lines of every disgraced actor or athlete who runs afoul, stares into the cameras to apologize, provides their **Environmentalists'** *mea* *culpa* to Oprah, and is forgiven. These are not examples of becoming **Environmentalists** to utilize charity to build a brand but more of trying to put a spin on negative effects as a result of their organization. Getting involved to help, regardless of the reason, isn't necessarily a bad thing but be careful if you or your brand assumes that we the consumer aren't savvy enough to see through your thin attempt.

Now having said that, some of the companies that create disingenuous cause efforts to mask their involvement are not necessarily "evil" in their attempt to win back some favor.   It's not to say that we cannot give them a little credit for their attempt to be crafty marketers and spin doctors who try to distract the community from the issues.   Just know that playing the "cause" card comes with ramifications if the brand isn't forthright.

I speak to college students regularly (yes, there goes your hard-earned tuition money, Moms and Dads) and I often say that if I ever get a resume from someone at *RJ Reynolds* or similar, I'd hire them on the spot. Why would someone like me who has never smoked a cigarette in my entire life and is vehemently against that horrible habit so quick to concede to work with someone who promotes it, you ask?

It's quite simple from a business perspective and it has almost nothing to do with the millions of dollars the tobacco companies spend on their (tax-relief) pro-social campaigns. It's merely the fact that if the tobacco marketers can generate billions of dollars in revenue each year despite having to market a product that says *on the very package* that the contents may (or will) kill you or turn your lungs to mud, then those must be some pretty savvy marketers.

It's one thing to be in the water surfing when a large shark happens by. It's another thing entirely to *paddle out* when you know a large shark is there! These guys know they have a deck stacked against them but still fight the marketing fight every day. I wouldn't do it myself, but I recognize when someone has the ability to succeed with extra odds against them.

Going back to the *GM* cereal discussion, with childhood obesity at an all-time high, it's no wonder that children's cereal brands also want to get in the fight and "help reduce' the epidemic. They want to at least give off the perception that they care about little Johnny's health. They give millions of dollars to the cause and provide impressive amounts of resources to groups that want to fight the ongoing battle of overweight kids. (Helping them to get healthy, not actually fighting against fat kids). Except for the obvious...

Reading countless PR articles about the donations and support the large breakfast cereal companies produce all seem to be missing a key point... Aren't these organizations producing products that one could argue not only doesn't provide a solution, but are actually part of the problem? The amount of sugar in these products can't possibly be void of all blame in the epidemic. Not many nutritionists I know encourage you to eat two big bowls of *Fruity Yum-Yums* before going on a run! When the Mayor of New York feels the solution is banning the larger size soda and not the soda itself, they are fighting the symptoms, not the disease. (FYI, if giant diet sodas are outlawed in NY, then you won't see *this* addicted surfer in Manhattan any time soon.) But like the *BP* discussion earlier, are these groups "helping" a cause or trying to limit their blame in the epidemic they are directly involved with?

I don't want to pick on these categories or products in particular and in fact, some have actually changed their ingredients to be *better* than their previous fructose-flowing formulas. But it goes without saying that creating a cause marketing effort because your brand has a black eye isn't in the spirit of the *Surfriders* or the author of this book.

Dove dishwashing soap donated substantial amounts of product and other resources to help wash thousands of birds during the *BP* disaster in the Gulf. The liquid soap product is a logical solution to help out and *Dove* was more than willing to step up and lend a hand. *That* is a great cause marketing effort. Relevant and logical.

But if you are the PR lead for *BP*, don't tell us how great it is to be able to help *Dove* sell millions of dollars of product in return for washing down baby seals and other Gulf Coast animals you have hurt. Keep the PR to the spinsters that have no choice but to try to turn a situation around. Keep the pro-social marketing efforts to the brands that want to make a difference and utilize the cause platform to advance a community first and foremost. Not cover their tails.

To get away from the cereal section on Aisle 4, I'll provide another flimsy cause marketing effort that I've experienced and can't quite seem to swallow. It demonstrates one of the two points we are discussing, that you can't be part of the solution if you are part of the problem...

How do children's television networks honestly claim they care about our youth as they allude to when they run the annual campaign to encourage kids to turn off the TV for an hour and go play outside? They want to help the health of our children by getting them to turn off the tube for an hour. But by their very nature, unless it's one of the exercise participation-type networks (that we all have watched before without participating in a single push-up), television executives actually *don't* want kids to do anything else *but* watch their product! And of course purchase the products the sponsors buy ad time for.

In fact, the instructions to "turn off the tube" for an hour or a day is really 100% *opposite* of what they spend all day, every day working for you to avoid doing for the other 364 days of the year! Let's be honest, if the network really wants to encourage kids to get healthy, how about going dark *twenty-four* hours a day and allow the pudgy little children to get in much better shape?

They want to have a positive face (albeit a chubby-cheeked, overweight pre-teen) on the obesity issue and while in actuality their product most likely contributes to the stagnation, these TV execs think they can position themselves as a solution instead of the problem with a weak, one-time cause effort. While I do applaud any attempt to try to do the right thing, if it doesn't succeed, then why do it? And if your haphazard plan is to do a one-time boycott of your product but return a little later to resume bad habits, is that really a solution?

But enough of the negative cases! Some *Environmentalists'* philanthropic tie-in's work and are exciting and some don't quite move the needle, but it's apparent that more often than not, most of the successful cause marketing efforts can be traced to a sound foundation of my two postulates; good causes and logical reasons to support the cause.

Having spent most of my career in or around sports, I frequently come across athletes who have a foundation or charitable interest they support. Many have a reason for their particular effort and most tend to be a personal story that has lead them to support a certain cause. Players who put forth a champion's effort can often utilize their celebrity or status to generate millions of dollars and/or significant awareness for their cause all for the sole purpose of making a difference. In essence, they are producing successful cause marketing efforts utilizing themselves as the brand and doing a better job than classically trained marketers.

Up until the doping confession, Lance Armstrong was as well-known for the *Livestrong Foundation* and his battle to fight cancer as he was for his seven-time Tour de France wins. He made himself a brand, had a relevant and compassionate story as a cancer survivor, and the tireless effort to promote his cause for no apparent reason other than to win! While the breakdown of his story and character are devastating (see the STARFISH chapter for more on Armstrong), I ask that you take the philanthropic element at just face value for a moment. The millions of dollars raised, the huge awareness he garnered for those fighting cancer, the yellow rubber bracelets. As a stand-alone case study, the *Livestrong* effort is monumental and companies jumped at the chance to join a huge effort that was draped in good intentions. Lance may be a cheater but the results of *Livestrong* are 100% legit!

Certain marketing tactics overlap and you will see much of that in the areas of ***Environmentalists*** and ***Starfish.*** Many celebrities (***Starfish***) have their own philanthropies to give back or at least put themselves in a positive light and they are often examples of either what to emulate and what not to do.

One of the athletes I have had the pleasure of working with in the past and seeing first-hand in action is New Orleans Saints QB and Super Bowl MVP Drew Brees. As a past winner of the NFL's Walter Payton *Man of the Year* Award for his charity and character, Brees is as passionate about his philanthropy as he is about scoring touchdowns (well, almost). And if you replace #9 with Pepsi or Ford, you would have a huge corporate marketing success case study that any senior level suit would be proud of. The Drew Brees example follows the main fundamentals of a successful charity; the cause is powerful and the story supports it.

Among the causes that Drew's *Brees Dream Foundation* supports include the *American Cancer Society, Rady Children's Hospital*, and *Building Through Brotherhood* where his fellow fraternity brothers from various colleges are sent to New Orleans to help rebuild Katrina-ravaged areas. Each of these charitable endeavors serve a great purpose and relate directly to the Brees "brand" and his relevant experience because Drew has ties with San Diego and New Orleans. By being a citizen and athlete of those communities, he has been personally affected by loved ones afflicted by various ailments (including former teammate Steve Gleason's bout with ALS), personally visited the disaster area of Katrina and spoken with hundreds of affected local residents.

I had talked with Drew about the creation of some of his cause efforts and we discussed, as a Sigma Chi fraternity member from Purdue, how he wants to serve as a stellar example for the younger college students of today. He combined two of the elements in his life, his loyalty to his fraternity brothers and his new town's disaster plight and worked to develop something that would benefit both in the *Rebuilding thru Brotherhood* effort. The result of his campaign brings undergraduate Sigma Chi fraternity members from around the country to volunteer in New Orleans to help rebuild the community. A brilliant way to mentor, provide his **Starfish** power to a cause, and make his adopted town stronger.

While charity and cause efforts are not mandatory and are truly a moral decision to get involved with, the Brees example is a great study in how you can build incremental awareness and distinguish yourself from your peers. I'm sure Drew didn't get involved with all the noble causes to look good but as a byproduct of his hard work, integrity, and passion, he has established himself as one of the top athlete givers in our society. And if others want to sing his praises and highlight the charity that he and his wife champion, I'm sure he wouldn't object!

There are no limits to what a good philanthropic campaign can do for a brand. Hell, if you only look at the actuals of a campaign (the tax write-offs, impressions garnered, and branding opportunities) it's a positive effort for an organization. And that's only if your Mr. Spock-like Finance Director has no emotions or ability to look at the greater good your efforts provide. Companies tend to worry about the bottom line first and foremost and if you can generate awareness, buzz, goodwill, and even revenue while doing something positive in the community, then you can appease everyone.

Being an **Environmentalist**, able to give back in the form of awareness, support, finances, or other resources is the cornerstone of a well-rounded business. At the end of the day, if you are able to utilize your product to support a charity then you have earned a victory. I'll be the first to admit that even though some will argue that it's the "commercialization" of the charity or "grand standing" by the corporate partner who demands some sort of gratis in return for a contribution, having your logo on the golf tournament banner or having the CEO interviewed dishing out pie at a homeless shelter is a very fair price to pay to make a difference in the community.

The public has come to expect a little showmanship for the donation but a small amount of credit seeking is fine as long as it doesn't start to overshadow the good that is being generated. I'm not providing a political platform with this book nor do I advocate one side or the other between the Republicans and Democrats, but the flack that Vice Presidential candidate Paul Ryan received last Fall is a prime example of **Environmentalists** gone wrong. But it gives us a look at what a superficial effort looks like and how it can backfire.

Showing up at a soup kitchen for a photo op that would surely make the candidate look good, Paul Ryan was so transparent and disingenuous with his attempt that it backfired. Ryan stayed for a total of fifteen minutes by some accounts, threw on an apron after the chores were completed, and took it upon himself to be photographed washing the *clean* dishes! The workers in the kitchen were later interviewed (after all, Ryan invited the media there) and they told the aspiring VP not to do dishes as they were already finished. It was a pretty big snafu and took what could have been a good attempt to lend a hand and turned it into a strike against him. Wonder if *BP* took credit for bringing the dish soap there too?

We often trade assets for charitable needs and whether it's giving a thousand *Reeboks* to a homeless shelter so they have shoes or *Comcast* cable running 300 spots promoting a *National Geographic Channel* cause marketing effort, the end result is that there is a distinct benefit to the philanthropy. If you are able to gain in some form while giving back, then that's a quid-pro-quo that any marketing mind should see as a positive exchange.

While these easy communication and PR stories will garner exposure, you can also incrementally drive more interest for your good will with greater accomplishments. A story giving back one thousand units is good but ten-thousand is better and so on. As a result, when aligning your cause strategically to ensure the charity is viable and can truly make a difference with your efforts, supporting an issue that your brand endemically stands for makes for a very powerful cause marketing campaign.

ENVIRONMENTALIST

SURF LESSON

How Can I Help?

Some lessons are not difficult to learn or apply and it's more about just focusing and doing it, rather than learning some ancient tribal secret. The SURF LESSON for this chapter is rather simple; who do you want to help? Referring to our earlier discussion about making sure your cause is relevant and effective, let's look at what your organization, product, or service does on a daily basis and who you could help in the process. Take a moment and answer/discuss the following:

A) Our organization's main brand or item is....?

B) Currently, we either do nothing officially on the philanthropic front or we have X or Y as our cause marketing focus.

C) If the Red Cross contacted us to contribute to helping a group in need, we would most align with....?

D) What would be the best way for those in need to utilize our product to better their situation and how can we make that happen?

E) Is our best attribute the ability to provide a product/service, financial support, or awareness for the cause?

F) How can we maximize our impact on the cause and (as a for-profit company) ensure that we receive acknowledgement, exposure, or other value for our genuine and sincere effort?

Like any somewhat cynical reader, you may want to review my qualifications to advise fellow marketers on the various areas of discussion. Beyond my somewhat novel take on associating surfing with marketing, I do have a successful track record in all of the areas I have highlighted in this book. Besides my experience in creative marketing (see TOW-IN SURFING), I would put my cause marketing passion up against anyone's in the profession. I have been associated with non-profit work my entire life as my mother spent much of her professional career with the *Muscular Dystrophy Association*. As far back as I can remember, I was participating in some form at the various events and fundraisers *MDA* produced. Sure looking back on some of the "fun" activities my mom had me perform as a child, including sending me as an 8-year old roller skating all over town distributing event flyers or swimming in algae-filled public fountains collecting coins at shopping malls, might be red flags by today's child labor laws but in the 70's and 80's it was just considered helping the cause. I did learn a great deal about how to communicate and succeed in the non-profit space in the process. And boost my immunity to pond scum.

Because of the sensitivities by nature, I quickly learned that the commercialization or self-promotion element via a non-profit organization is a very fine line. The difference between successfully dropping into a seven-foot face on a wave and falling over the top of the falls can be a fraction of an inch either way and navigating an association with cause marketing is just as sensitive. You can be aggressive in what you would like to earn in return for your brand's involvement and have set goals, but you also need to ensure that the measurable marketing results are not the primary motivation.

I can say from experience as ***Environmentalists***

that there are pros and cons to promoting your brand in this manner. Personally, I have experienced the thrill of victory as you help a wheelchair-bound youth play in a summer camp basketball game that they would never have been able to experience otherwise and see the fruits of your labor come to shine. Unfortunately, I have also been on the wrong end of a cause marketing efforts when presenting the large novelty check for an event I championed. During the Labor Day Telethon in Los Angeles, host Casey Kasem mistook me (as a thirty-five year old fully-grown man with a goatee) as one of "Jerry's Kids" on live TV!

But while I make light of my experiences, I speak from the heart when I reiterate that while most companies do seek some form of awareness, positive PR, exposure, etc. for their efforts to help the cause, I believe that the general public will allow for some leeway and leniency if the greater result is helping make a difference. At the end of the day, if one food bank receives enough donations to cook meals, or one more injured child gets the needed prosthetic, or one house gets rebuilt by Drew Brees, then feel free to brand the effort with your corporate logo because you've made a difference.

ENVIRONMENTALIST

CASE STUDY

JOIN THE *T.E.A.M.*

Speaking to college students about sports
and entertainment marketing is a
rewarding opportunity where my passion,
case studies, experience, and lessons
have been able to motivate various
undergraduates to pursue the exciting
and fast-paced world of marketing.
Building off of that notion, we developed
*T.E.A.M. (Tomorrow's Entertainment &
Athletics Marketers)* that utilizes these
lessons and helps educate and motivate
at-risk students in the inner city of Los
Angeles. The philanthropic goal behind
T.E.A.M. is to simply provide inner-city
students the exposure, resources, and
confidence to stay off of the streets and
work towards their dream careers.

For some reason, most marketing and
advertising agencies are exempt from the
social obligation to give back and while
their clients may have established
charities, and the clients' retail partners

have philanthropic causes, the agencies themselves are often able to fly under the radar.

Based on my aforementioned experience, I sought to develop *T.E.A.M.* as a way to give back to the community based on our strengths. Just as *Tide* has the successful *Loads of Hope* initiative where their mobile experience helps displaced residents and disaster victims to attain the basic humanity of clean clothes, *T.E.A.M* helps communicate what *we* as an agency do best; creating interesting campaigns.

With a solid curriculum that features industry guest speakers and real-world assignments that we utilize in our campaigns, *T.E.A.M.* exposes students in some very underprivileged schools to the skill sets and talents needed to succeed in our industry. By bringing in corporate partners for different levels of participation, my agency successfully leverages our *T.E.A.M.* philanthropy in our community as well as helping advance their exposure and good will.

Each *T.E.A.M.* session has the students participating in actual campaigns and we teach the high schoolers about the fundamentals of a good ad campaign or marketing strategy while having them create everything from headlines, copy, or sweepstakes concepts. Allowing the students to try their hand creating a *Los Angeles Lakers* promotion or developing a campaign for *Fox Deportes* has been an amazing success in terms of building confidence.

Allowing me another vehicle to communicate with my clients (without always selling my agency's capabilities for the billionth time) is a platform that we have certainly taken advantage of in return. Engaging Corporate America to allow inner-city students to participate in the development of their marketing and advertising initiatives is a simple, yet effective, philanthropic partnership that benefits hundreds of members of the *T.E.A.M.* So if the partners help out by having aspiring marketers work on their brands, and *T.E.A.M.* is able to captivate at-risk students and show them options in life, and my agency garners a unique reason to reach out to the clients, then call us the *Patriots* or the *Yankees* because we have created a winning *T.E.A.M!*

"Once you're a surfer you're done. It's like the mob or something. You're never getting out."

– Kelly Slater

CHAPTER 7

TROJAN (SEA) HORSE

The headlining tactic of this chapter refers to the famous wartime tactic and we will explore uses of the *Trojan (Sea) Horse* along with several other ways to successfully infiltrate a market or category. I would much rather use surfing vernacular than war references to discuss the art of marketing, and while business is often discussed in more dire terms of combat, we will choose to communicate marketing's great philosophy of gaining a foothold to provide continuous future dividends via nautical examples.

Marketing, by definition is the activity, set of institutions, and processes for creating, communicating, delivering, and exchanging offerings that have value for customers, clients, partners, and society at large. When I refer to "infiltrating" or "persuading" or the concept of manipulating/influencing consumers, retailers, or clients, I am not implying that we use "bait and switch" tactics or communicate untrue aspects of our brand. The surfing culture is a very inclusive *Lifestyle* and more often than not, they will welcome outsiders and rookies so long as you steer clear of the key spots (see the BIG WAVES chapter). But, when a kook rolls in and tries to act like he has game or thinks he's a long-time local, it's easy to smell a rat. Wannabe surfers who drive their shiny new SUV around town with a $2,000 top-of-the-line board on a rack yet never drop it in the water (or has ever waxed the board for that matter) often have unfavorable results and are quite easy to sniff out. I liken them to a product that is promoted to have quality X when in fact it really isn't as good as advertised or doesn't even have the capability to address the marketer's claim at all. Many of the weight loss or supplement products fall into the exaggerated or unregulated claims and tend to prey on the basic human emotion without really being able to confirm their claims. Ultimately, we want to highlight our strengths, communicate a favorable story, and promote our brands in the best light but we must also be honest and ensure that while we may be telling a larger fish tale, we do have an actual fish on the line.

Earlier I mentioned our action sports network launch featuring skate, surf, snowboarding, and BMX. We needed to be true to our audience and as organic as possible. Teens and 'tweens who engage in the action sports lifestyle are very fickle and savvy and we discussed how imperative it is to understand and assimilate to the target *Lifestyle*.

The network effort is a great sample of how you need to be organic in how you communicate to your audience. We created a 22-city skateboard tour that went around the country with pro skaters and talent including Ryan Sheckler and Wee Man to promote the network (refer to the CASE STUDY in the LIFESTYLE chapter). We had a huge turnout because we were able to provide desirable entertainment, star power, and a "wow" factor that had the organic feel that the kids could relate to. It didn't appear forced, it wasn't *"your father's skate demo"* and it wasn't a school assembly at lunchtime. But ultimately it was a *Trojan (Sea) Horse.*

The tour was subtly sponsored by a major network service provider. The thousands of teens and 'tweens that showed up to watch the demos, meet their favorite skaters, and even compete for a chance to participate in the *Gravity Games* on national TV were exposed to the new network and quickly demanded to receive it. And while this was one of our main objectives, to build awareness for the network, the more subtle goal was to get them to request it with the provider so they could watch it. The audience goes to the event for A and leaves promoting B. ***Trojan (Sea) Horse*** 101.

Another example of finding any method of entry possible and how a ***Trojan (Sea) Horse*** technique can be utilized involves our work with a major corporation's communication strategy. We were approached to create simple B2B internal e-mail blasts that were not profitable and not very sexy. While some internal staffers wondered why we would spend time on a project that would be considered philanthropic if not for the billion-dollar client, we saw it simply as an opportunity. Bring in the ***Trojan (Sea) Horse***!

We entrenched ourselves with the group as the champion of a smaller project yet it allowed us to have an on-site presence, be seen, and most importantly, be privy to conversations and strategies that would prove to be significantly more than simple e-mail blast projects.   We were now abreast of all of their upcoming projects, direction, and future marketing efforts. While we signed an NDA and would *never* provide or discuss the information outside of our team, it didn't mean that we were not able to be exposed to their marketing strategy and future opportunities as a solution or resource. Our plan to simply be involved with the group and stay on the top of their mind allowed us to be positioned for the larger projects we desired. It may seem simple to make yourself available but one of the key principles of the **Trojan (Sea) Horse** is to get inside any way possible to attain a larger goal.

Getting into the users' line of vision is the ultimate goal of any marketer and then the up-selling, repeat business, or even new communication to a willing audience can be executed much more effectively once you are in. *Gillette* is an example of a **Trojan (Sea) Horse** product that executes the strategy to perfection. They often give away a new razor to consumers and then turn a significant profit when the customer continues to purchase pack after pack of the blades that go with it. While I don't know if my razor needs the 4 blade, 8 blade, or Edward Scissorhands attachment that some NASA scientist has apparently developed, I do know that I would never purchase a competitor's razor because I already have my *Gillette*. So I continue to be a well-groomed lemming and purchase new and improved refills of the same blade I've had for a decade. Like my face... the strategy is smooth.

Whether you are an agency, restaurant, or product, you are always fighting to keep your hold on your position. You need to be on the shelf, inside the client's office, or in the prime real estate just as surfers fight for position and anchor themselves in the ideal spot in the lineup. So using one vehicle to unleash a secondary stronghold is a proven method to keep yourself ideally aligned and on the inside track for greater awareness, sales, and revenue.

While working for a CPG company, I once hired an agency to build a promotional database so we could track all of our promotions in real time. Until that point, we had used an excel spreadsheet posted on a shared-drive. Sure it doesn't seem innovative by today's methods, but a decade ago when we were still posting a database of entrants on a public drive that always seemed to be either erased, unformatted, or screwed up as many times as the amount of people using it, it was groundbreaking. The *Trojan (Sea) Horse* case study became apparent when the small agency developing and managing the back-end suddenly became needed across all projects. They sold their capabilities as a back-end solution which was their strength and soon they infiltrated the front-end and were doing *all* elements of the promotions. Originally, they sold us on the database (which was perhaps 10% of the total project) and the ability to utilize any other agency for the consumer-facing elements including concept, creative, etc. Now, they wouldn't ever complain about just doing the back-end *but* time and time again they would suggest their creative or provide solutions based on their exposure and growing familiarity of our products. Before we knew it, somehow it was easier to just have them do both the front and back of our promos so we didn't have to bring in multiple agencies for every activation. That infiltration and subsequent stronghold on the group's promotions is still intact today and now that I am on the agency side and calling on my old team, I can't break that stronghold! Bad for me, good for them.

There are often subtle differences between the various strategies we discuss in *The Surfer's Guide To Marketing* or multiple tactics incorporated into one effort. Just like a small shift in weight on your board will change your direction, slight adjustments in the variables will change the approach we use. While the **Remora** (see the REMORA chapter) discusses symbiotic marketing where both parties benefit, the **Trojan (Sea) Horse** focuses more on creating a presence or smaller foothold when you have no traditional port of entry. While it's not untrue or deceitful, the entire concept of the *Trojan (Sea) Horse* is designed to allow you to infiltrate a market, category, or position that you could not normally become involved in by using one method to achieve another. Just like a ten-year-old skate punk has no interest in discussing which television provider they get their channel from, we provide a common link (via the action sports network's desirable content) that at least allows us to enter the picture. Get a seat at the table (or skate ramp) any way possible.

Philanthropy (discussed in the ENVIRONMENTALISTS chapter) often falls under the umbrella of a *Trojan (Sea) Horse* approach and depending on the goals and tactics, it can be a great resource when other avenues are non-existent. While we all want to give back and provide successful cause marketing efforts to help others, we explore the benefits, approaches, and secrets of leveraging philanthropy as a marketing tactic more in other chapters.

The digital platform is a great opportunity to roll out a *Trojan (Sea) Horse* tactic as it's a simple entry with tremendous upside. Badges, for example, are a great way to get you brand out there with the ultimate goal of growing into something larger. Users love to have their website or social media filled with awards, badges, or icons that identify them as "special" or having experienced a product or cool brand. Simply put, they wheel in the **Trojan (Sea) Horse** into their laptop "courtyard" and before you know it, you are able to provide them offers, services, and favorable content that grows your positioning. Please don't think that I mean Spamming. Like every human, I detest Spam and I'm not saying to drop a cookie and blast every bad product offer out there to the unsuspected user who happens by. I mean providing good, relevant content or offers to those who show a passion for the brand and have welcomed your logo into their world.

Writers/bloggers who link to articles or create favorable content around your brand or service often have an ulterior motive aside from patting you on the back. Their goal is to gain more exposure for their own product by promoting your name favorably. Companies that are so determined in the new age to have "consumer feedback' and favorable impressions from the social media space will jump at anything positive about their brand.

Bloggers are for the most part smart (although you might be thinking of using terms like pessimistic, antagonistic, and catty). They understand that corporate suits *don't* understand. Recent positions from blue-chip brands like *Coca-Cola* state that a favorable post or a "Like" online is significantly more important that old school impressions or traditional ad reach. Bloggers are very willing to set out a *Trojan (Sea) Horse* story that they hope will get picked up by large groups. Like the common cold virus, eager corporate PR and marketing reps take the story and blast it across their significantly larger audience which actually exposes everyone to the blogger. Brands are happy with the good press from an "authentic consumer" even though it may not be sincere or genuine and really, they are actually growing the bloggers' awareness by exposing them to the millions of consumers/followers that the big company has.

Another example of a *Trojan (Sea) Horse* might just be closer than you think. Do you really think I'm bright enough to write a book? If you have read this far, your answer is "probably not" and if you know me personally, then the "probably" becomes "definitely". But I was bright enough to create a vehicle that provided authentic and informative content... which also basically serves to promote my marketing talents and my agency over and over again. Often times, shamelessly. I want each of you with marketing opportunities or those searching for dynamic solutions to utilize the tools and tactics in *The Surfer's Guide To Marketing* to succeed. And as an award-winning agency, I'm here to help and easily accessible!

"If in doubt, paddle out"

- Nat Young

CHAPTER 8

TIDE POOLS

When viewing today's market place in terms of the different ecosystems within the ocean, we can draw analogies to the various categories of life, fishes, reefs, storefronts, plants (both aquatic and industrial), or e-commerce. At this point, I've hit you over the head with so many surf analogies that you should be able to reach parallels between your unique marketing conditions and different oceanic topography. We discuss various approaches to achieving different marketing goals, explore how to fight with larger competitors (**Sharks**) or how to swim in high-profile currents, and even ways to utilize your strengths to appear larger if you can't in fact actually get bigger.

While most marketing groups want to own the category, be perceived as the marketplace leader, or just out-sell the competition, the truth is that there is an ecosystem somewhere that provides you with the best opportunity to survive. There may be many you can do well in but ask any retailer or business pro and there is the "ideal" position that would be their first pick.

There are many factors to look at beyond where you ideally want to be and I tell clients not to get too hung up on only being in the center of the middle shelf on a grocery isle. Where you currently are might be a great position or perhaps your **Tide Pool** may be shrinking due to economics or change in trends and you need more options.

It's important to evaluate your space, ensure you are not in a shrinking **Tide Pool** and most of all, find the ideal niche for you to operate in. So now, we present a discussion on **Tide Pools**, or finding the alternative marketing channels for your brand.

I assume everyone has been fortunate enough to walk on a beach, visit a tropical location, or at least take a trip to *Sea World*. The shallow, rocky areas that host a wealth of diverse sea life are a great representation for finding alternative areas of distribution or commerce. The overwhelming majority of sea life and diversity, somewhere in the 80% range, live near corals, reefs, and similar structures. While blue whales and whale sharks can navigate the open ocean, there are millions of smaller players that have adapted in different surroundings to survive and thrive.

If you were to walk along a rock formation and see the various shallow puddles, cracks, and crannies, you will quickly realize that there are hundreds of unique plant and animal species in these areas, and even more areas to hunt or hide in. A small snail might not do as well swimming in the deep blue sea but on a wave-battered rock, the little guy can eat, drink, and do whatever it is that snails do.

Your business may be the snail in a **Tide Pool**. Or a sea anemone. Or sea urchin. Or gobi. Or some other small creature. As the sea urchin says, *"you get the point."* We can't possibly write a marketing book that covers all areas of business and addresses every relevant problem or opportunity that every brand faces. Brands and companies, like fish and sea animals, come in all shapes and sizes, utilize various tactics to survive, and experience elements unique to their particular ecosystem.

But if we take the time to look at alternatives to the wide-open ocean where the big fish swim, we may be able to carve out some niches that allow you, like the little snail, to hang on and live a fruitful little life. By taking some of these alternative opportunities, combining them with some of the proven strategies we've discussed, you could create a unique opportunity that might have you positioned as the apex predator of your *Tide Pool*. And as you grow and thrive in each smaller *Tide Pool*, you may be able to trade up to a larger pool with stronger competition, and larger returns. Even the biggest *Shark* starts off as a smaller baby and gradually grows. The key is to find the starting *Tide Pool* or if you are more established, the ideal *Tide Pool*.

Let's explore some of the basic ways *Tide Pools* differ and survive in the ocean environment. And through this Sea World-friendly discussion, you will be able to see patterns in the marketplace that best align with your brand. We will discuss large and small ecosystems, the different tactics and survival strategies that the sea life uses, and how these platforms or philosophies can help you flourish and establish a stable market.

High Tide Zone

These zones are the typical landscape you envision
when thinking of a **Tide Pool**. Exposed during lower
tides, the animals, plants and rocks are subject to
greater risks and danger than when they are protected
by water. Along with the typical risks associated with
being a sea anemone, hermit crab, chiton, or other little
shoreline critter when submerged in the ocean, the
High Tide Zone creates greater exposure when the surf
diminishes and even more variables like sea birds, sun,
and grabby little kids enter the equation. I'd like to think
of these **Tide Pools** as the "fringe" markets or lower
rent districts. The animals (products) tend to be
smaller, have greater risks of survival, less continuous
resources like waves bringing oxygen or food, and
overall work harder to survive. Due to a lower cost of
entry, more popular category, or just plan volume, these
markets are where most of the hard-core, basic
competition for survival occurs.

The independent retailer lives primarily in the *High Tide
Zone*. They have no support other than what they
provide for themselves and while schooling fish find
safety in numbers, the stand-alone restaurant or retailer
needs to be nimble, omnipresent, and creative if they
are going to survive. If they look to the hermit crab who
outgrows his shell, abandons it, and moves into a larger

one as a symbol of adaptation and flexibility, then they can follow in the same claw-steps in the market place. While the significantly busy marketplace of independents that dwell in the *High Tide Zone* live almost day-today with more variations of **Sharks** (competition), it is the majority of small businesses that would live in these shallow pools. Less security, less resources, more things looking to take you out.

Does that sound like a new product or a garage start-up trying to claw for resources to compete? These market place conditions are a reality and while they provide more challenges, there is a way to survive and even flourish in this market. If a sea star can grow, move, eat, and reproduce while exposed to the above-ocean conditions, then your brand can also adapt and thrive.

Low Tide Zone

Housed deeper in the sea, the *Low Tide Zone* is under water significantly more than the previous **Tide Pool** and only visible at low tide. There are distinct advantages to being submerged more of the time including protection from the aforementioned land predators. Another key is the constant channel of resources available. Just as the tide brings nutrients to the muscles, snails, shrimp, algae, sea cucumbers and other deeper water varmints, an established marketplace provides incrementally more resources. These tend to have more robust, more established animals (or brands) that have less numbers, more size, and take up significantly more market share per capita than all of the *High Tide Zone* counterparts combined.

Think of *Low Tide Zones* as shopping malls or mass retailers. The cost of being housed in friendlier, traffic heavy **Tide Pools** is advantageous because the infrastructure is in place, co-op advertising promotes all of the shops/brands in the facility, consumer traffic is significantly greater than if you were a stand-alone retailer, etc. There are many benefits to being in a more established, large-scale tide pool and while the animals or brands that reside there tend to be larger, able to fight back, or better supported, it doesn't mean that they too don't have significant obstacles to overcome. There are still constant threats from larger predators like seals, fish, and other animals that patrol deeper waters. And there are always adaptable residents from the *High Tide Zones* trying to undermine your predators like smaller **Crabs** who want to steal your food (like those little stand-alone mall carts that pay significantly less rent and still capitalize on the traffic that larger anchor stores drive and pay to obtain.)

In looking at which direction your company would like to establish their niche, as a smaller brand available in the

High Tide Zone with more obstacles and less resources or as a more established *Low Tide Zone* resident with more opportunity but a larger buy-in, we should explore how we can utilize the previously discussed tactics to create a obstacles habitat.

One more key area to discuss is the open ocean. If *Low Tide Zones* and *High Tide Zones* represent independents and group retailers, then the ocean represents the marketplace as a whole. Open oceans can provide a "clean slate" of opportunity that might create hybrid marketers that adapt the best practices of both **Tide Pool** levels or create their own ecosystem. Just as a mass of seaweed in the open ocean attracts smaller fish who hide under the protective cover, or a sunken ship can develop corals, fish, and a virtual reef where there used to be sand, the open ocean allows dynamic marketers to create their own story, develop their unique resources, and often times break out of the traditional channels.

Add to that the e-commerce tsunami that has rolled in, and there is a constant churning of competition and opportunity. Our goal is to help the little crab on the rock or the half-exposed sea star to successfully live in the ecosystem that fits them best. By exploring what elements your organization has at their disposal and what features and benefits of each **Tide Pool** provide, we can answer the "Place" of the "Four P's" formula.

TIDE POOLS

SURF LESSON

CHECK THE TIDE

I am going to ask you to create a list of the various pros/cons your business or brand has and first help establish where the most advantageous **Tide Pool** is for you. After we determine which ecosystem is the ideal positioning, then we can discuss some of the marketing tricks or strategies to flourish.

Ask yourself the following questions and refer to the strengths and weaknesses that the available **Tide Pool** locations offer. You should be able to draw a somewhat sensible conclusion as to where you need to be based on distribution, demographics, resources, and other variables.

> A) Where do buyers
> look for your product

or service? Is it best to be in a single retailer or multiple locations?

B) If they look in a store, what kind is it? An independent boutique or a large supermarket? Or both? What about e-commerce? Or via a catalogue/direct mail?

C) How can you access the right distribution channels?

D) Do you need a sales force? Can you promote at trade shows? Make online submissions for distribution? Sampling?

E) What do your competitors (**Sharks**) do, and how can you

learn from that and/
or differentiate?

What do non-
competing brands in
the desired market-
place do?

Once you have figured out which channel might be the
most advantageous based on similar brands that align
with your answers, we need to see what previous
strategies apply to your survival. Is it best to latch on to
a larger partner a la the *Barnacle* or make yourself
loom larger like the **Puffer Fish**. Again, I can't answer
all of your questions but I can help you start to map
your plan.

Looking at our marketplace analogies, let's focus on the
open ocean which involves the total combination of
Sharks (or competition), resources, opportunities, and
threats. If we can survive as little sea crabs in the total
space of our world, then we should be able to flourish in
more of a niche area, right?

Customers are the plankton of the ocean. Everything
basically hinges on the billions of organisms that feed
everything from tiny little anemone to the huge blue
whale. Everyone in the sea needs nourishment and it

all starts with the ability to bring in customers. They are the lifeblood and nourishment for our business and are crucial for survival.

Once we identify what type of plankton we are looking to attract (knowing your demographic and ideal target market is a basic Marketing 101), we integrate that into the inventory of our assets and strengths which we've previously outlined. Be sure that you don't simply list assets, target markets, etc. but truly analyze them.

Like a survivor washed up on a deserted island, you need to be resourceful with everything you have. Can you use a small mirror to signal a ship or start a fire with the sun instead of just looking at your castaway five o'clock shadow?

Think about your pricing, product components, marketing mix, etc. and see if there might be unique areas to adjust. Can you become the "low price" product in the market and gain share? Could your event that has traditionally been seen as a niche movie theme become a more mainstream general admission activation? Does the predominantly male-targeted product you make have opportunities to expand the line into female or youth markets? All of the things that you have access to can be explored to see if there are new uses or different groups of plankton to attract.

And just when you think we have all of the traditional channels to attract and feed off of our plankton, along comes a huge, misunderstood, unlimited potential of a resource to engage the plankton... social media!

We touched on digital and viral elements in several other chapters including how to utilize the platform for a **Puffer Fish** or **Trojan (Sea) Horse** tactic but now it's time to discuss the overall social media benefits and myths as they apply to helping you entrench yourself in the chosen **Tide Pool** you wish to swim.

For anyone over 40 reading this book, don't be afraid that the social media wave is too big and you've missed your opportunity to catch a nice ride. And for anyone in their 20's or 30's who thinks that because you "grew up" on *Facebook*, Tweet every meal you eat, or have tons of *Pinterest* boards, you now think you are ready to sit at the CMO desk, calm down grommits and let's approach this from a *marketing* perspective. Lastly, for the more "mature" marketing executive, let's not think these young surfers are qualified to run Apple because they have the iPhone 3, 4, 5 or (insert this month's number here) and talk in gigabytes and version 8.6. I tell senior-level marketing clients that they wouldn't let a 15-year-old kid write the copy for a full-page 4/4 color ad in the *New York Times* because they know how to type so why would you trust your social media communications to a JuCo dropout with three nose rings just because he can Tweet? Even though you may not be the most savvy social media expert in the office doesn't mean the traditional principles of branding and communication don't apply.

Utilizing social media is a great way to communicate your brand. At the time of this book, we have all become well-versed in *Facebook* and *Twitter.* (Hell, my 70+ year old mother "Friended" me the other day on *Facebook* which officially means I now have to officially shut down my account.) For those of you a little more integrated, you may use *Pinterest* (so everyone can see the shoes you find "adorable") *LinkedIn* (*Facebook* for people who wear big-boy pants) or even *Flickr*, *Instagram*, or *Google +* (you want to upload things to multiple sites in case your buddies didn't see it the first three times). It gives instant access to potentially millions of flowing plankton AKA customers. But as I warned you in the discussion about viral video, just because you may have access doesn't ensure you will reach them. And if you do, what do you say?

Think of social media along the lines of the **Remora** in terms of the relationship dynamic. It is a mutually beneficial, two-way street and if you don't understand, just like the guy who buys a foam surfboard at *Costco* and heads out to a 10' break the first day he tries to learn to surf, you will not last long. Social media is a dialog that allows brands to communicate *with* their customers as well as *to* them. You can provide significant impressions, consumer favor, and revenue if you develop a solid, engaging communication platform. Never before has the customer had so much influence in instantaneous timeframes. And in turn, the marketer's opportunity to learn about your brand's perception directly from the target is huge!

A great way to stimulate sales and traffic, utilize social media to reward your customers. If you can provide occasional discounts, promotions, etc. then they are more likely to stick around. Creating innovative content, worthwhile and relevant information, and exclusive access or breaking news are ways to keep your fans or followers engaged. As important, listen to their feedback. You may not be able to please everyone, and you certainly cannot turn on a dime and create a new beer-flavored gum line just because @TomTom176 suggested it, you can measure the pulse of the *Tide Pool* on a fairly regular basis. We used to rely on agencies to survey consumers or create focus groups and by the time marketers gauged the *Tide Pool,* the tide had often shifted and the beach was dry.

One interesting CASE STUDY that I will now present involves the "next step" of the process. Once you have a good temperature, what do you do with it? Do you acknowledge that our marketing world is fluid and social media has brought instant rip tides into the equation? We no longer have a one-way tide (brands). We have a rip tide effect with consumer feedback that causes ebb and flow. There are great examples of what dynamic groups do to utilize feedback and solidify their spot in the *Tide Pool.* And sometimes there are wipe outs...

TIDE POOLS

CASE STUDY

GO F- YOURSELF!

Sometimes we can learn what the best tactics or strategies are by watching an epic fail! I learned pretty quickly about the shallow reef over at the Palos Verdes cove from a kook who dropped in on a six-foot face onto six-inch water-covered rocks. And just because I am using *Tide Pools* as an analogy for marketing conditions doesn't mean I want to actually surf in them!

Two television networks in the fall of 2012 were having carriage disputes with the cable providers. The two sports networks couldn't agree on a fair rate with the local cable systems so they did not appear on the channel lineup. Sports is a key passion of Americans and I often say that it's such a powerful vehicle, it can get grown men to wear NASCAR driver Mark Martin's race apparel, even when it had a huge *Viagra* logo across it. *"Sure I'll wear a giant E.D. advertisement as long as the #6 car ends up in Victory Lane! Yeee Haaaw!"*

These are what I refer to as "Passion Brands" that go beyond identifiably and have embedded themselves into our emotional thinking. *BMW, Mac (Apple),* and many of the aforementioned sports brands come to mind and if you don't think these are "Passion Brands" note the level of excitement a *Mac* user has versus a *Dell PC* user when describing their laptop. A *Dell* user seldom screams about how cool *Windows Office* is but the average *Mac* junkie is quick to tell you how amazing their *iPad, iPhone,* iPorn or whatever they use is. Borderline brainwashing.

Back to our case: In an effort to generate fan support for these two different television networks, both of the respective marketing groups took a similar approach to social media. Thinking they could waltz in, post some aggressive comments about the operator who refused to carry the service, and rally fans to their cause, these two channels had no idea that they just paddled into a school of barracuda wearing meat-lined wetsuits!

The comments from the passionate users who were unable to get their favorite team's game on TV due to the dispute were obvious. Cyberspace tends to get pretty tough and mouthy (when the user is hiding in a basement 3,000 miles away) and I'm fairly certain the snide responses are much more aggressive than if the person was standing face-to-face with you. It's like the time I was surfing and may have "accidentally" dropped in on a 15-year old kid to snake his wave and afterwards he was a little too chippy. He cursed me, splashed me in the face (which I still don't understand because I was *in* the water and already wet), and threatened me with a little bodily harm. I often think of that spoon-fed kid from some Orange County gated community as the stereotypical blogger because he talked a great game about "taking me out" but when it came time to possibly do something, he simply paddled away with visions of grandeur in his bleach-blonde head.

Now imagine thousands of fans like this punk looking to spew negative comments, combined with the genuine fans whom are irate that they don't get their favorite games and are looking for answers. This perfect storm is not afraid to let their cyber-opinions be heard!

Network A decided to do nothing and not inform the fans of the league they acquired rights for in an effort to avoid engaging in dialogue. Their approach was to be radio-silent and not disclose many updates or news about the network. As you can imagine, before the network had even launched, there was already a negative association and distaste for the brand. People had (fairly accurately and astutely) called out all of the shortcomings and negatives about the new network before they had even aired a single game.

In a last minute effort to try to quell the social media beating, rather than address the issues and inform consumers that the games they want to see will not be on, they simply tried to engage fans as if nothing was wrong. Ever see a surfer at the bottom of a huge wave at Teahupoo as it's crashing down and he is not in a good position to get out? You know he's about to get crushed but you just can't stop looking....

"(NETWORK A), are you kidding us? You take our soccer rights and then ask if Lionel Messi is the best player?! That's all you have?! (NETWORK A) needs to give up the rights and get out of the TV business" posted one fan. "You suck!" complained another. And so it went for 173 posts and counting. Surfboard flying one direction, body flying another, ten

tons of ocean blowing the network up! To quote the reporter witnessing the 1937 Hindenburg disaster, *"Oh the humanity!"*

Network B tried a little different approach when its fans questioned the inability to watch their team due to the network and cable provider bickering. While similar negative, frustrated posts were being generated by the minute (including several that included a demand for the network execs to do something that I think is biologically impossible) they thought they would take action and offer a Facebook promotion. Instead of doing nothing, perhaps a small giveaway will solve the ill-will that was brewing.

And you know what happened? THE EXACT SAME THING! But doesn't every social media "expert" say that giving away free crap will make users happy? Sure, if you don't have any real world faults or shortcomings that need to be addressed. I'm the first to recommend engaging content, rewarding fans with free premiums or products, or provide them some recognition for being loyal. It's a proven way to maintain current fans and cultivate a pleased demographic.

But if you have a serious PR nightmare, you can't simply put a little band-aid on a shark bite and expect it to heal. They needed to utilize the social media forum and slowly engage fans, answer their concerns organically, and develop a solution-based dialog.

The advantage of the social media platform is the ability to create dialog and provide honest, transparent, and real answers. Not throw out a free T-shirt and hope that the millions of people who are on Facebook at any given time forget their ire.

While all of the other CASE STUDIES in this book end with tangible, positive results by utilizing the tactics we discuss, I felt it was important to emphasize the need to treat social media like any other platform. You spend many hours, a ton of manpower, significant dollars, and other resources towards traditional mediums so don't assume that free media doesn't need strategic direction, sound communication, and artful handling of those instantly reachable fans/followers. Hey, if the beach at Teahupoo is free and open to the public, why do you need prepare and train when you can just paddle out for the first time and position yourself right where that last surfer's body parts are floating?

Social media offers a dialog for you to engage users on a level that we've never experienced in the past. Social media is not as easy or as hard as you think and there are several simple steps I adhere to in order to create an authentic, and successful campaign.

Rather than just have one chapter on social media with some brilliant ocean analogy, I purposely broke it up into smaller discussions across multiple subjects. The main reason is simply that many of these tactics are integrated across multiple platforms. For example, **Environmentalists** use charity as a **Trojan (Sea) Horse**. Social media can make a **Puffer Fish** appear larger and also serve to help you secure your **Tide Pool** to live in. It's important to know that marketing strategy utilizes many touch points and a sound strategist can utilize similar resources to advance unique objectives. Just as I encourage you to use creativity in all elements, social media can serve as a solution for many marketing opportunities.

TIDE POOLS

SURF LESSON

SOCIAL MEDIA IS "LIKE" THIS

This is a simple checklist of tactics to incorporate when creating social media engagements. Because digital now allows for seamless flow between the various **Tide Pools** and open ocean markets, smaller fish and giant tuna alike can thrive if they follow simple guidelines.

1) CREATE YOUR VOICE- Make sure that the tone and voice of your tweets, posts, pins, etc. are on brand. If you are a lighthearted, casual brand, then you can add some humor. If you are trying to be a bold, edgy brand, ensure that all posts and engagements reflect the brand's position and not the social

media representative posting on your behalf. Stay in character. Take a moment and describe your brand's voice. Perhaps align it with a celebrity for tone/attitude. Are you more of a Vince Vaughn or Morgan Freeman?

2) PRIORITIZE - It's important to list the key messaging you want to get across in order of importance. Social media allows for fluid conversations and in addition to answering or creating dialogue, it's important to ensure your main talking points get communicated. List your top five talking points in order.

3) FREQUENT CONTENT - Having a *Twitter* feed or *Facebook* page that doesn't have continuous, relevant information isn't going to garner attention. Keep it updated and commit to having content! Create a calendar of set points, frequency of posts, and "wild card" spots that get filled with real-time topical discussions or replies.

4) IMAGES - Along with your updates, open-ended conversation starters, promotions, etc., you need to integrate images, infographics, etc. Keep it interesting for the users and they will respond favorably. Images and unique elements get retweeted, "liked", and forwarded more than copy alone. Select a half-dozen images to start with, add them to your schedule, and ensure that you have a percentage of graphics, videos, and images to post.

5) INCLUDE LINKS - As we discuss in this chapter, we are creating your digital footprint. Traffic is measured in the amount of integrated users you can create and who comes from where. Adding links and subsequently being linked will increase your exposure and drive your social media platform. List the other sites, feeds, brands, retailers, etc. that you would like to link to/ from and ensure they are on the social media schedule.

6) REPLY - Make sure you answer a

good portion of your followers and create engagements that create dialog. Answering questions or highlighting loyal followers will provide favor with the consumer and show that it's a portal to communicate with the brand, not just another company selling their services. And your response will get retweeted by excited users.

One thing you can count on about marketing is that you can't count on anything. While proven strategic marketing plans may have a higher percentage of success, it doesn't mean that by following the rules you are guaranteed to have your brand become a household property. It takes timing, resources, and a little luck to succeed in the competitive environment. Sometimes, a single path is not the only solution.

If a surfer is at a break where the waves form a nice right over and over, he can assume that he'll most likely pop up and head that way down the face. More than likely, it will be true. But, there are always factors that might make him adjust his line from the shape and size of the wave, positioning, other surfers, etc.

The same can be true when discussing which eco-system, or **Tide Pool** you wish to live in. Sometimes, you can move from one to the other, create your own open ocean market, or find advantages in multiple markets. There are times where a large fish chooses to stay in a smaller ecosystem and has adapted to that market for whatever reason. The epaulette sharks of Australia are much too large to lurk in the super shallow reefs and tide pools they dwell in and often find themselves in water too shallow to even swim. But, unlike a large store with significant overhead, inventory, and employees that doesn't bring in enough revenue to stay afloat, the epaulette is like a small brand that is agile and has adapted the ability "walk" across reefs to find enough water in shallow pools. This little guy will squirm across rocks and has evolved to survive in a space it shouldn't really belong. Again, the exception not the rule.

You can always adapt and move to the most advantageous placement but it's always better to analyze the ecosystem and make an educated approach. The message being that finding your appropriate sized **Tide Pool** will allow you to flourish while being in the wrong market makes you... wait for it... a fish out of water.

TIDE POOLS

CASE STUDY

WAHOO'S OWNS THIS REEF

Certain brands just gravitate to a sensible market. Large-scale consumer package goods do well in *Low Tide Zones* like grocery stores. They sit on the shelf and get gobbled up by thousands of consumers. Other brands take a big fish in a small **Tide Pool** position.

Wing Lam, founder of *Wahoo's Fish Tacos* is a leader who prefers to "own the **Tide Pool**" rather than share. *Wahoo's* philosophy is simple; They don't want to get lost with other brands and if they can't own the event, then it doesn't make sense for them to be there at all.

I met with Wing (over some yummy fish tacos, of course) and he listed several events centered around surfing competitions ranging from little grom contests to *Association of Surfing Professionals* events where *Wahoo's* is the predominant brand on-site and more importantly, visible to those watching on TV, online, or other secondary methods that drive impressions.

If there is an opportunity to integrate the *Wahoo's* brand at these surf events, the the So Cal eatery will own the **Tide Pool**. They don't want to share sponsorship, have a small presence where they simply serve up tasty treats, or have a small logo on the poster with other brands. They dominate the signage and the entire **Tide Pool** is marked by their branding.

While the general rule of thumb is to be a smaller business in the shallow *High Tide Zone* market and larger brands competing in the bigger, deeper Low Tide channels, *Wahoo's* participates in events where they are the big tuna among smaller fish. They don't have their logos on Super Bowl ads, or look at **Big Waves**, but they choose to be where there ideal demo (young, active beach types) gather and go full force to ensure they are the only fish there.

The company's philosophy allows them to bring their branding and support to events where they will be the predominate brand. And as **Environmentalists** they do also support local initiatives and often do fundraising events with 20% of proceeds going to the school, team, etc. to help give back. But their mantra towards which *Tide Pool* they want to dwell in is simple... bigger fish, smaller rock because we own this reef!

"As for my own surfing, let's just say that when the waves start pushing 10 feet, I get this tremendous urge to make a sandwich."

– Bruce Jenkins

CHAPTER 9

BIG WAVES

Surfing is the ultimate combination of preparation and improvisation. You can plan out your surf day, check the tides, the weather, surf reports, and even scout locations. Wax your board, pack your wetsuit, and even get a little pre-session nutrition.

Surfers study breaks to determine the best directions, spots, and best possible techniques. Noting who is out there, how crowded it is, and what the overall vibe feels like. Again, surfers engage in all of the basic skills that a marketing expert does, only scanning the horizon instead of the marketplace. Rocks instead of store shelves and undertows instead of rebates.

Once they paddle out and place themselves in the ideal position, the preparation stops and the improvisation begins. The best laid plans of a surfer dropping in on a large face breaking right goes out the window when another surfer takes the same line. Or snakes your wave. Regardless, you are forced to alter your plan for a wave, a set, or the entire session based on factors that perhaps you either may have foreseen or had no way of anticipating.

If that sounds like every marketer or businessperson's daily struggles, you are not alone. Vince Lombardi said "*Failure to plan is planning to fail*" and that adage rings true until, despite countless hours and dollars dedicated to R&D, competitive analysis, and other marketing tells, you get thrown for an unexpected loop by your client, the competition, or worse, the consumer.

The more competitive the environment, the more confident and seasoned a surfer or marketer needs to be. Let's face it; a guy from Idaho who has been out on a surfboard a few times isn't going to try to paddle out at Pipeline. And if he does, tell his next of kin that he just wasn't prepared. It's about understanding your (or your brand's) capabilities, resources, and preparation to handle variables both expected and unforeseen. And even then, as surfing legend Greg Noll quoted at the beginning of the book, even the big dogs can be surprised with what they are able to pull off. So if *they* have doubt, what runs through the head of the small business owner or weekend surf warrior?

I equate Pipeline in Hawaii where the greatest surfers in the world can be humbled as the blue chip, grocery isle. The *Nestle's, Pepsi's, General Mills*, and other A-list brands dominate the shelves like a great white circling seals. During the key buying times like the holidays, these pinnacle spots become Pipeline or Mavericks on a huge day! The best in the world take on the greatest waves nature can create. If you are strong enough to challenge the most competitive consumer markets and fight toe-to-toe with *IBM* and *Apple* on a regular day, do you have the extra gear to keep up the fight during huge surf days with **Big Waves**?

People often refer to the consummate event, activity, or occasion as the "Super Bowl" of said category. The biggest American sporting day and one of the world's most watched events is indeed the ultimate surf spot on the ultimate day. Instead of wind, swells, and tides all creating the perfect storm, it's the media, grandeur, celebrity, and sometimes even the teams on the field that make this the Super Bowl of marketing. To paddle out and compete with other top ten brands during the Super Bowl is to enter a **Big Wave** classic on an epic day.

If I had a dollar for every client that has expressed interest in having a presence at the Super Bowl, I wouldn't have to spend my time hawking marketing books. It's obvious that everyone wants to be at the "grown up" table during Thanksgiving and the Super Bowl is as big as it gets. And large brands like *Budweiser, Doritos*, etc. (the Laird Hamilton and Kelly Slaters of the marketing world) belong on the biggest stage and spend significant resources to gain significant returns. It's high stakes at its best and the ultimate **Big Waves**.

But is it the right model for every company? For your brand? More than likely, no. As a casual surfer, I know there are some spots I do well in and some conditions I can handle. I don't have the skill, experience, or let's just say guts, to try to catch a tube at Mavericks when it's 25 feet high. That would be a bad business move.

Rather than even try to get there, the majority of organizations (and even several who you would think *could* survive) shouldn't waste valuable efforts or resources when odds are that a huge wipeout is looming.

When developing a marketing strategy for my clients, I always ensure that an honest, strategic evaluation of their limits are incorporated. While everyone would like to have the record-setting amount of eyeballs on their brands that the recent Ravens-49ers Superbowl earned, let's be realistic. These huge locations and the swells are for the pros, not the groms. The parties, activities, and other on-site elements that surround Super Bowl week, while more affordable than the game itself, are also in a battle to outshine the biggest, most identifiable, and deepest-pocketed companies out there. So unless you make a significant dedication, you will get lost in the expensive clutter. Just like trying to go up against *Mattel* during the holidays may not be a smart business model for your basement-built toy company, people in our position too often think with their heart and not their head. Sure, everyone wants to earn millions in revenue during the Holiday season but are you spending incremental money that doesn't move the needle when you could be selling twice as much in July for half the cost? While there are ways to maximize your brand, company, or opportunity with limited resources (revert to the PUFFER FISH chapter), a huge day on the North Shore is not the place to learn how to surf. **Big Waves** are only for big riders.

So how do most companies compete?

Simply paddle out into a spot that you are familiar with. Understand the conditions, tides, and crowds at the spot you feel comfortable with. If you have faith in your abilities (or your brand) in the marketplace you have selected, enjoy a fun session. Perhaps the waves are not too big, the tide is coming in, and the water is warm enough for you. The competition is minimal, the price of entry is less than larger retailers, or perhaps your brand can communicate its message in this smaller environment. Have visions of a barrel ride in clear warm blue water of Tahiti while you enjoy a cold winter Pacific ankle-slapper in Redondo Beach. Catch your waves and be happy without wishing you were on **Big Waves**.

There should always be a dialog in your head that weighs the resources against the reward. For example, near my house is my favorite surf spot known as *The Cove*. While the waves are beautiful and fun, there is significantly more effort involved in getting there. You need to hike down a long hill and then paddle way out against the surf to get to the break. It's taxing and a lot of effort. But the reward is a large wave with a really fun, long ride. Meanwhile, it's significantly easier to jump in down at the beach and not have to walk or paddle much. But the waves are smaller, wall off onto the sand, and are not nearly as fun. Less resources used to get there but less payoff. It's your call as to where you think you should be. As you know, we explored the different markets in depth in the TIDE POOLS Chapter earlier in the book and here we are focusing on diving into the deep end with **Big Waves**.

But, if you want to compete with the biggest **Sharks** on **Big Wave** days, that's what we are here to discuss. You will note this is probably the shortest chapter in the book as not many people want to spend millions of dollars during peak times if they can leverage the other tips and tactics to better balance out their marketing mix. But, you wanna go big so let's do it!

After you select the right **Tide Pool** environment/ market, you plan out your line. I can pretty much only go right most of the time because I'm not good enough to steer when I'm facing the other direction and going left. I'm willing to admit that if I had my ideal wave, it would be a small, right breaker that allows me to sail down the line. Easy, not much skill or prep other than to get in the right position. But the waves, like the marketplace, do not always give you the perfect little ride. I pop up, it's a left breaking wave and I am forced to adapt my stance, turn my board, and head to the left or wipeout into a cloud of whitewater. Again, no matter how much I was ready and how prepared I was, sometimes you have to adapt. A surfer in your way, a wave going the opposite direction, a rock, a slip of your foot. You get the picture.

It's not *if* you adapt your approach but what you do when you inevitably have to. If you have heeded my advice and selected a break that suits your surfing abilities, the adjustment is less dramatic. You understand the break, understand your variables, and have the confidence and skill to make a bottom turn and keep going. The huge **Big Wave** days (or Super Bowls or Thanksgiving's Black Friday) are not the place to make unsure decisions that could have you biting coral within a matter of seconds.

But when you do find yourself in popular surf spots on larger days, what can you do? Are there opportunities to actually get a wave, and even pull off a nice ride? Of course. Nothing is definite and even when you decide to surf with the big boys (despite my warnings and common sense) you can indeed survive. *Sometimes.*

I call one of my favorite tactics the *Zig-Zag*. Simply put; if they expect you to Zig, you Zag. It's cutting back and forth on a wave, changing direction. When common sense tells you to climb the wall and get out of the wave, maybe you can pull off an Arial and drop back in for an epic ride. It's all about finding a creative approach, unique messaging that differentiates you from the crowd, and having the abilities to pull it off. Surfers and marketers are often referred to as artists for their ability to carve out a ride or a campaign that seems obvious only in hindsight. And Zigging when the competition is Zagging is the easiest way to break free from the rest of the crowd and leave your own unique mark on a *Big Wave* day.

BIG WAVE

CASE STUDY

COMIC BOOK CONVENTION

Comic Con in San Diego is one of the big days at Pipeline we discussed. The "Super Bowl" of fan-based entertainment, the convention attracts hundreds of thousands of entertainment fans and media representatives from around the globe. The biggest entertainment companies in the world converge to promote a new Brad Pitt movie or the next *EA Sports* video game or *Star Wars* product. And when our client, one of the top blue chip entertainment organizations in Hollywood wanted to build buzz without having as large a budget as people would come to expect, they needed a creative solution. They wanted to surf the **Big Waves** without the big budget.

For those of you who have never experienced Comic Con in person, it's exactly as you may imagine. While I don't profess to understand why people want to dress up as Superman or Darth Vader (or worse; the guy who dresses as Gilligan from *Gilligan's Island* to apparently express that his alter-ego in costume form is a nerd as well?) the convention is basically A.D.D. on steroids. Lasers, masks, and many beautiful models manning the booths wearing skimpy, sexy outfits. It's a spandex and latex lover's dream come true.

In my humble opinion, it's actually quite a cruel exercise having beautiful women interacting with nerdy guys who have never even touched a live female much less held a conversation with beautiful models! But, they stare at the booth staffers like a killer whale watches a seal on the beach... unable to get it but just praying for a chance.

So with beautiful models in skimpy outfits everywhere, how do you stand out and draw the attention towards your booth? We had a very clever approach to do exactly the opposite of the majority of the vendors… have the brand's support team wear *more* clothes!

To differentiate their models from the rest and emphasize one of their office-based television programs, the girls were outfitted in a conservative wardrobe including branded shirts, long grey professional skirts that went below the knee, and conservative pumps. They looked like professional office employees (if your office was full of models). The Brand Ambassadors were attracting attention based on their beauty *and* their unusual attire. We had stories and images appearing in publications around the world highlighting the unique angle. It's the ultimate irony when you are in an environment where business suits are unusual and capes and boots don't even cause a reaction!

The results were better than expected as the group of professional looking, attractive models caught everyone's attention and made the display the water-cooler talk of the convention.

Some brands cannot avoid being in the huge surf of **Big Waves**. It's perhaps a limited market controlled by giants or perhaps a single entry point. At that point, you can do the same thing everyone else does to keep up, or create a better story. For example, airlines don't have many variables to compete with that their competitors don't have. They all take off from airports, do basically the same service, and have access to the same resources. So how do big brands like *United* or *American Airlines* compete on the **Big Waves** of LAX or JFK? And how could someone come in and reinvent the science of air travel to make a move?

Singapore Airlines was one of the innovators in the airline industry for years. They were the first to offer free headsets and a variety of meal options. They also focused on inclusion of the various perks with regular and economy class to provide a distinction from the competition. While other airlines were squeezing their customers, *Singapore Air* was offering more. They added *KrisWorld* as one of the first in-flight entertainment options that allowed users to have access to over twenty videos, twelve video games, audio channels, etc. They realized that while the general service of getting travelers from A to B is limited in the competitive airlines war, they could make sure the experience during the service was unique and superior. It's a great way to gain an advantage in the apex competitive environment *Big Waves*.

BIG WAVE

CASE STUDY

LIKE A VIRGIN

Taking the airline experience to the next level, *Virgin* has completely blown away the competition by utilizing what I consider classic marketing elements. If the **Big Wave** marketers are competing in a tight surf spot with huge visibility, then

Sir Richard Branson is the guy who shows up with the hottest new design on his board.

Branson and *Virgin* look at the marketplace, especially on those **Big Wave** days or markets and determine what the competition is *not* addressing (sound like an innovative Aussie from our TOW IN SURFING chapter?) They analyze the opportunities, listen to consumer feedback, and study trends that the other **Sharks** (competitors) in the market don't see, don't want to address, or don't care about. By doing the little things better, capitalizing on the bigger things where they can actually make a difference, and brining a fresh, innovative perspective and energy, *Virgin* is able to create a place in the **Big Wave** lineup.

When discussing how *Virgin Airlines* was able to jump into the water with the big boys, Branson was quoted as saying, "*In 1984, when companies like Pan Am, TWA, British Caledonian and British Airways ruled the skies between London and New York, Virgin Atlantic started off with a single Boeing 747. But by 1991 British Caledonian and Pan Am had shut down, and TWA followed 10 years later."*

All brashness aside, how could he bring an upstart, single airplane operation in and bring the established giants to their knees during constant **Big Waves**?

Branding. Simply put, *Virgin Airlines* is what I refer to as one of those *"Passion brands"*. Like *Mac* or *Nike* or *Starbucks*, consumers who are disciples of these brands spend more on the brand, increase loyalty, and tell more people about the positive elements. It becomes part of their belief that the product is superior and the branding/style is significantly beyond the competition. Taste studies had *McDonald's* coffee on par with *Starbucks* for a fraction of the price but the perception that *Starbucks* was better and stylish won out in the mind of all of the passion brand connoisseurs.

While *Virgin* focused on customer service and design, they added a whole new level of style to the approach. As I mentioned earlier with the Brand Ambassadors, the people who interface with your customer are the most important staff members you can have. So when *Virgin* set out to create a better service element, they started with the 'front lines". The people employed by *Virgin* go out of their way to help you, are overly friendly, and leave you feeling like they are there to say "yes" and not overcharge you or turn you away like the other airlines tend to do.

It's the same way that the teens who work at *In-N-Out* are on a whole different level compared to other fast food places. They are friendly, competent and make the experience much more manageable as you wait in line three-times as long as you would for any other similar chain. If your goal is to exceed customer expectations and provide a positive experience, it starts with the front-line staff. (Also, having the yummiest *Double-Double* in the business doesn't hurt either).

The customer service goes beyond the front line as well and too many companies try to put on a brave face only to have the rest of the organization fall apart. Rather than have a friendly face apologizing for your ineptitude, carry the "will do" customer service dynamic throughout the organization. Aside from the staff that greets you, the flight attendants who assist you, and the pilots who fly you, *Virgin* has great results for booking flights, on-time departures, and even baggage issues. Again, the experience is good but a friendly team that solves problems (or better yet avoids having them at all) bumps you up to First Class.

The other element that *Virgin* excelled at is "packaging". It's no coincidence that everything *Apple* touches is on-brand in terms of design. The sleek, stylish look of the products, the website, and the in-store retail locations all scream *Mac*. If you are a fan of the product, and you go online or in-store, you become immersed in the brand and raise your level of satisfaction from good to passionate. *Virgin* has added decor to help differentiate their brand and thus raise themselves up above the rest of the airlines trying to ride on **Big Waves**.

Airports are as sterile as hospitals and not very warm or inviting. Branson wanted to model his airline after his gregarious, stylish self, so by utilizing a hip design, he knew he could draw the user in and make consumers "engage" in his brand rather than just use it. Adding cool lights, music, slick furniture, etc. in the *Virgin* terminals instantly set the mood for a different type of airline experience. And with a little style and color beyond the boring layout of the competition, one would argue that the emotional level of the consumer rises and the passion starts to grow.

Virgin didn't really do anything new in terms of the actual travel service. They did it better. Cooler. Improved the experience, created a nightclub look/feel. And brought their airline from being just another competitor on **Big Waves** to the best brand out there when you want to pull off a 10,000 ft. arial!

The sum of the parts make *Virgin* a complete experience and serves to drive passion. If your flight is reasonably priced and arrives on time, and then on top of it you add a cool ambiance and style with friendly staff, you have exceeded the expectations of the consumer. The company has gone from a necessity (flying from A to B) to a commodity (doing it in style). And hence, Sir Richard knows that the *passion* of a brand is formed by consumers between what you expect and what you actually receive. Better than expected equals an increased passion. Less than expected puts you at the bottom of a very ***Big Wave***!

"I kind of quit surfing when I got out of high school, but then a few years ago I started to take it up again. I'm not an expert by any means, but it's so wonderful to get out in the ocean and get a different perspective on things."

- Actor Jeff Bridges

CHAPTER 10

STARFISH

While past chapters have touched on the use of celebrity to influence brands, this chapter is all about **Starfish**, or the use of famous and not-so-famous spokesmen. Earlier I used the example of *"Be Like Mike"* as the *Nike* slogan that sold millions of shoes. It's a great example in a very succinct phrase but it tells volumes.

By now, you don't need me to spend time on discussing why brands use spokespeople to endorse their product. You get it. But what we will focus on in this chapter is *who* to use and *how* to use them. It's not as easy as you may think and not as automatic as you might imagine. Just having a local team's player signing autographs at the retailer isn't a guaranteed formula for success. So the **Starfish**, those famous Kahunas of the surf lineup, are not always a simple solution to drive sales.

I have had the pleasure of working with hundreds of famous athletes, actors, artists, and celebrities throughout my career. I have done marketing campaigns with such famous legends as Wayne Gretzky, Jerry Rice, Michael Chiklis and the aforementioned Mr. Jordan. I have also spent significant time with not-so-famous *Starfish* like soap opera stars, reality television characters, and more up-and-coming models than I can count. And the number one thing I look for in all of them, even with a huge A-list *Starfish,* is their relevance to the brand.

I book a lot of athletes for appearances and I enjoy getting to know and work with all sorts of amazing players from the world of sports. From NFL QBs to Baseball Hall of Famers to Heisman Trophy winners, I have utilized famous *Starfish* to drive everything from phone service to baseball cards to beverages. My personal philosophy when working with players is to treat them the way I treat my surf buddies... talk a little smack! I don't get too worked up over someone's fame or on-field accomplishments and maybe after all these years I'm a little immune to it. You simply need to be somewhat professional and not get too enamored with the talent, regardless of how much you admire or cheer for them.

Remember, **Starfish** are people too (did I just write that?) They have good days and bad days and different personalities that may not be what you see on TV. Just because singer Jordin Sparks is super sweet in an interview doesn't mean she is like that 24/7 (but she actually is) and just because Tony Romo is serious in the locker room doesn't mean he's always intense (he's actually a funny, smart-alec like yours truly). So don't get too caught up in the perception when handling **Starfish** and make sure you are only playing up their image in the campaign.

In fact I'm amazed at the people who get overly giddy working with talent, especially when they are the **Starfish's** point of contact for the promotion. My goodness, act like you've been there before! You coordinated his/her appearance so why are *you* flipping out when they show up to do the job?

Now don't misconstrue my callousness for apathy. I am

the first one to suggest using **Starfish** as a tactic to bring excitement, sizzle, and passion to your brand. I just want marketers to understand that those emotions are supposed to be reserved for the fans who we are marketing to!

When I explain how we use talent frequently and show some of the previous examples of an event with Marcus Allen or a radio commercial with Ashley Tisdale, people tend to think I am an agent or representative. I tell them I'm in a better position because I work with their people. I'm an agent's best friend because when I call, it usually means I have work for their client. I equate it to being a pretty girl at the dance because when I call an agent, my jokes seem to be a little funnier, I'm a little more handsome, and I'm suddenly more interesting... as long as I use their roster. Rather than commit to an agency that has a set list of players, I prefer to find the right fit for the job that best fits the client/brand instead of trying to shoehorn their existing list of guys into the role.

There are great agencies that provide **Starfish** and I have had many successful efforts with CAA, IMG, Octagon, Wassermann, and others. I just prefer to keep my options open and select the ideal spokesman that will maximize the relationship regardless of their representative.

When selecting talent, it is also important to avoid personal bias. I'm not just talking about a lifelong San Diego Padres fan like myself not booking Los Angeles Dodgers players whenever possible (ok, maybe once in a while I may be guilty of that) or getting too attached to a *Starfish* because you know them personally or have easy access to them. I have had occasions where we try to do something with an old baseball player or B-list actor who the head of the marketing department grew up with, only to find the event or promotion fall flat because the *Starfish* used wasn't a big draw or the right name. And the boss doesn't want to hear his pal stinks so inevitably *you* will take the heat for the shortcomings.

There are some easy choices to make when selecting *Starfish* and aside from budgets, availability, non-competes, etc., you don't need to be Jerry Maguire to recognize that a heavyweight star can bring awareness to your brand. Now Brad Pitt is as big as they come but I'm still not sure those *Chanel 5* commercials where he rambles on about God-knows-what were worth the effort or the reported seven large he was paid. Did that enhance the brand? Drive sales? Or did it make the company and the *Starfish* look a little silly? (Then there is what conspiracy theorists have claimed; that they did such a bad job on those commercials *on purpose* that it created more buzz and was much more talked-about than a straightforward attempt would garner!) That would be pure marketing brilliance if they really did torpedo their own ads but I'm guessing they just stunk. To quote the CEO of *Coca-Cola* when *New Coke* flopped back in the 80's and people wondered if it was a brilliant sabotage marketing ploy... *"I'm not that smart."*

Having Tom Brady with *Under Armour* or Taylor Swift promoting *Diet Coke* seems like relatively safe choices. Both are not likely to embarrass themselves or their sponsors, have significantly higher approvals and Q ratings, and are instantly identifiable. And those types of deals involve more zeros in the contract than I'll ever see so if the company has deep pockets, then it's a great deal. But for every Drew Brees and One Direction *Pepsi* deal, there are Lance Armstrong and Tiger Woods who appeared to be a sure thing only to ultimately bring negative association with themselves and the brands they represent.

It doesn't always need to be a huge ***Starfish*** either. Most companies don't have the budgets to incorporate big names into their campaigns. And that's fine. The ***Sharks*** that have multi-million dollar budgets will always be able to find the top talent like the championship MVP or Oscar winner and so I'm going to focus on ways to leverage ***Starfish*** for the small-to-midsize organization. Those who may think adding celebrity power is out of the realm of possibility but they might be able to create some star power within their resources.

STARFISH

CASE STUDY

WHERE THE HELL IS SCOTTSBLUFF?

One of the key variables in communicating to local audiences is the inclusion factor. A smaller segment or a finicky audience can be scared off quickly when "corporate America" speaks down to them. While a national overlay may work across the board and a **Starfish** that resonates on a national stage is good in general, if you need to address local issues on a local level, you need to see the world through your local consumer's eyes. Which brings us to Scottsbluff, Nebraska.

A national client wanted to establish themselves for a multitude of reasons, in smaller markets like New Berlin, Wisconsin and Scottsbluff, Nebraska.

They had an aggressive message they wanted to convey and there was concern that if we went straight ahead with the company's desired tone that no one would support them. They ran a serious risk of running people off with a harsh message that feel-good consumers didn't want to hear. So we needed a positive front to attract attention and subtly provide a soapbox for our client.

While marketers often use star power to promote our brands, bringing Derek Jeter or LeBron James wasn't an option for this project so we decided to go local. We didn't have the budgets or the ability to draw in super high-end *Starfish*. But as huge Nebraska Cornhuskers fans, we knew that we could bring local talent that resonated within that smaller market. Some of the *Starfish* that wore the red and white were perceived as much as royalty in Nebraska as other more prominent athletes were in New York or Los Angeles. So we created an amazing event featuring former 'Husker legends Roger Craig, Super Bowl running back for the 49ers, and Neal Smith, the Denver

Bronco's star which was the pro team of choice in the area. Great names in the state of Nebraska who were as big as The Beatles anywhere else.

While we were creating everything from our offices in Los Angeles, the promotion had to have a local Scottsbluff feel to keep up an authentic front. Subtle inclusion terms such as "we" and "our" help imply that we were locals and as much a part of the Cornhusker culture as *Bugeaters* and *Blackshirts.* So when giving the event location, we simply gave the location address and Scottsbluff, not Scottsbluff, NE 69361. *They know* they live in Nebraska and dead giveaways like the zip code imply that an outsider is responsible for their "local" event.

The results were better than expected as Roger and Neil entertained the record crowd and our client's story was told to 3x as many consumers as we had projected. And the huge turnout listened and absorbed our clients' messaging to the point of siding with our brand and successfully enlisting to help in the cause.

All while embracing *Starfish* who fit within our budget and resonated locally with the market we ideally wanted to reach.

Think through a campaign in terms of what the consumer wants. It sounds basic but too often, the train leaves the station and the original concept or direction has been edited by so many hands that the scope has changed. We once presented a concept for an open-mic comedy contest to support a sit-com launch featuring a comedian. We would bring in famous comics as our *Starfish* to build buzz. No brainer. The network ultimately had some unforeseen issues with the show we had concepted for but loved the idea so much, we were told to bring the comedic *Starfish* and the stand-up comedy concept they previously liked and had approved to a completely different spy drama. Huh?

If I was the ideal target market for a brand, what type of *Starfish* would excite me and motivate me to do whatever the challenge presented is? It's easy to put a top player with a shoe but what about toothpaste or insurance or a sofa line? Is there a way to leverage *Starfish* to cost-effectively drive your marketing efforts?

One of the trends that came along with social media

and Twitter in particular is having **Starfish** tweet on behalf of a brand. We are not talking about deals as a spokesman that includes on-air, print, etc. and significant dollars. We're talking about paying a Kardashian to mention your brand to her several million followers. And it may not even be a product the **Starfish** supports or understands, but simply cashes a check for the impressions like a human billboard or bus side.   Some of these have been so bad that now the FTC wants to have products tweet a separate blast informing followers that the **Starfish** is a paid spokesman. Recently, actress Kaley Cuoco was paid to tweet about a company's service and how great it was. Too bad the network that her television show is on happened to be in a large lawsuit with the company she tweeted for! It shows that we must be selective in which **Starfish** we present because all of the buzz generated from her recent tweets were all about the lawsuit and not the product she was pimping!

Conversely, if the great Laird Hamilton tweets about a new board, a cool exercise, or even an innovative and dynamic new hilarious marketing book utilizing surfing metaphors to communicate principles that is destined for the New York Times Best Seller list, it holds water. Even if you can cost-effectively get a **Starfish** to mention your brand, you need to treat it like any other medium. Weigh the overall impressions against targeted demographics. Does Justin Beiber and his millions of impressionable, young *Beliebers* (the "cool" term for his followers, if there is such a thing) matter if you are trying to sell life insurance? Do you want mass numbers or quality demographic numbers?

Recent studies have shown that celebrity endorsements can increase sales by as much as 20% and company stock as much as 25%. There is definitely a plus to adding **Starfish** and having incorporated celebrities into everything from on-air spots to packaging to appearances, I can whole-heartedly say there are benefits to doing so.

A unique way to integrate **Starfish** with their fans is via a new company called *CHATOGRAPH*. The company allows fans to "reserve" a chat reservation with a celebrity and then, along with their engagement with the **Starfish**, the user receives an autographed transcript of their interaction. It's the next wave of monetizing social media and utilizing *CHATOGRAPH* to bring famous athletes or actors to your brand, conduct a one-on-one engagement and then incorporating a memorabilia element is the type of cost-effective social media tactic that any brand can incorporate. It allows social media and celebrity to directly promote your brand as you can "sponsor" the *CHATOGRAPH* session or even "host" it on your company's website and social media pages. Check them out on *Facebook, Twitter*, or at *Chatograph.com*.

So if the question is not *why* use **Starfish** then let's go explore the criteria for *which* **Starfish** to utilize.

STARFISH

SURF LESSON

WISH UPON A STARFISH

Every brand is different and requires a unique voice, positioning, and style. You speak to unique audiences and segments so we need to ensure that we all understand there is no one surfboard for every condition. The next star might not be the right star. So let's explore some of the criteria for adding a **Starfish** to your roster.

1) Define what your brand is and what you want to say. We won't touch on this much here because we've pretty much surfed that break over the last several

chapters. Write a few key words that your brand would demonstrate if it was a human being. Are your shoes cool, sleek, stylish? Is your vacuum cleaner reliable, easy, and quiet? Whatever your brand identity is, make a note of it.

2) Who are you targeting? Again, we've gone down this road previously but we need to identify if we are look at an upscale, cerebral demo or a fanatical, face-painting everyman?

3) Credibility. Knowing that **Starfish** are human, we can start to target athletes or artists that have the similar characteristics as your brand or appeal to the target. Similar to the previous chapter on **Environmentalists**, this association must be true and relevant. Michael Jordan can promote *Haines* because he wears underwear (I'm assuming). But would he be a good *Head & Shoulders* pitch man since he's

bald? Probably best saved for
Troy Polamalu and his flowing
mane. The credibility of the
Starfish is key to persuading the
consumer to follow the spokesman's lead.

There are two parts to credibility;
the *Starfish*'s perceived honesty
and probability. The first is simple;
would a consumer believe the
spokesman? Are they honest or at
least *appear* to be honest? If a
convicted felon appears on TV and
tells you the hamburger shop
down the road is great, do you
automatically believe him?

The second-half of credibility is the
consumer's impression that the
Starfish is an expert in his field
and the brand they use is a factor.
Their perceived expertise or ability
to excel in their field while possibly
using said product is a key to the
story. Halle Berry is beautiful
and she probably uses the makeup
she promotes to get there. It's a

capable story that the consumer can associate with. Does the identity, credibility, and expertise of the brand and *Starfish* intertwine? If so, highlight those names and continue

Take the brand attributes and the human characteristics we've listed in Step 1 and Step 2 and start to list appropriate *Starfish* that could support both columns. Don't worry at this point about unique factors like cost, accessibility, etc. We can eliminate those later.

4) Now in the most vapid, vain line in *The Surfer's Guide To Marketing...* is the *Starfish* attractive? While it's a no-brainer to have a beautiful supermodel promote makeup and clothing, a pitchman must skew high on a physically attractive scale based on the most primitive laws of attraction. I previously discussed how our Brand Ambassadors need to meet a level of criteria that

includes physical appearance because countless consumer research has the targeted demographic responding more favorably to those who they rank higher on a scale of attractiveness.

While there are exceptions to every rule (Ask anyone who knows my beautiful wife and wonders if I'm holding her hostage in our marriage) the rule of attraction, combined with credibility, and awareness form the basis for your **Starfish.** Check your list, highlight the ideal **Starfish** who are still on the roster and now you know who would be an ideal representative for your brand.

5) Reality. Even though Hugh Jackman is your ideal representative and his looks, honesty, and multi-talented acting and singing abilities would make your restaurant or clothing line a huge hit, is it feasible? Many **Starfish** are not inexpensive and

there are "levels" that you need to stay within if you are a smaller company or brand. An MLS soccer player in your market would still drive traffic at literally one-hundredth of the cost of getting Wolverine to appear. After all the exploration of the right celebrity for your brand, there needs to be a realistic look at what you can afford and the logistics of using the **Starfish**. Perhaps the national star or league MVP mirrors a similar type of player on your city's team that will have a great impact. Replacing an Oscar winner with a reality star might fit both your brand and budget. Explore the limitations and see if your ideal **Starfish** is able to swim with your brand.

There are many formal and informal rules about using **Starfish**. For example, the "Rule of Six" applies to most Player's Associations for professional sports leagues. This rule simply states that if you use an individual athlete for an endorsement, then you can work directly with their representative. Once you use six or more players, it becomes a Player's Association play where you will need to work with the respective PA on the deal.

For those of you who wonder why they show an athlete in a different color, non-team uniform, it's because the company has secured the rights to the player but not necessarily the league. For example, the NBA owns the rights to the logos, marks, team names, uniforms, etc. but a company can hire an individual player without going through the league or team. So Shaquille O'Neal appearing in a generic white uniform is simply their attempt to mask the non-league partnership. Personally, I'm not a fan of having players in faux uniforms as it tends to look cheesy if not done well.

We did a large promotion for pro football where we couldn't use current players or teams so we utilized retired Hall of Fame legends and used a sepia tone design so the players uniforms (with no logos or marks) looked almost historic and not so much like a knock-off jersey. It can be done but it needs to be just right to avoid a consumer disconnect. So when the legendary football **Starfish** did the on-air commercial, they were in their civilian clothes and not a knock-off uniform. It doesn't make sense for a player who has been retired for ten years to be in a helmet and shoulder pads anyway and we wanted them to look as cool as possible to make them meet the SURF LESSON criteria of attractive, believable, and congruent.

Yet another key factor in selecting **Starfish** for an endorsement opportunity is the celebrity's playing status. Current players tend to have significantly more obstacles in doing business than retired icons. First and foremost, they have the "day job" i.e. their sport. It's much harder to book surfer Kelly Slater when he is going from town to town (or country to country) competing. Plus, his/her focus is on competition during the season. The off-season, when the **Starfish** have a more relaxed schedule isn't always that flexible either. With today's sports environment, the pros tend to be on the clock all year long between OTA's, free agency, off-season conditioning programs, etc. Save for a much needed family vacation here and there, and the players' full-time job is in fact a full time job!

One more factor in determining between current and former athletes is the fact that teams have relationships as well. Noting the previous Kaley Cuoco example, just because the **Starfish** may not have a direct correlation with a brand, their parent company, team, or league might. When Dallas Cowboy's owner Jerry Jones announced a deal with *Pepsi* even though *Coca-Cola* was the league's official sponsor, they were not too happy. While I'm no legal expert (or even a writer according to some people) I could see where that might ruffle a few feathers! Every professional league prohibits current athletes from being involved with alcoholic beverages so don't even think about tying in a player with your new vodka or micro-brewed beer line.

Side-note: I do find it just slightly ironic that current professional players can't be associated with what my kids call "Mommy's Happy Juice" yet it was recently announced that beer sponsors just exceeded the $1 billion mark for sports sponsorship! And even worse, alcoholic beverage sponsors put their marks and logos all over NASCAR including on the actual vehicles because there is no better logical partnership than booze and cars! But I digress....

It's important when doing your homework that you ensure there are no conflicts between brands that a **Starfish** is involved with. Now they might drive a BMW and still do an autograph session for a Ford dealership but it shouldn't be a blatant, disingenuous relationship for fear of not meeting the criteria for selection as previously discussed. It definitely helps when a **Starfish** does enjoy the product as it lends authenticity and their enthusiasm and passion will show.

The all-time winningest goalie in MLS soccer history, Kevin Hartman, is a fan of *ZICO Coconut Water*. He drinks it and enjoys the taste and electrolytes that help him recover from his workouts and games. So it was a no-brainer for us to have Kevin get involved with *ZICO* on their team of athletes as he enjoyed the product and would praise it's value long before he was an official partner. Getting Kevin on the team was easy as he is an honest consumer of the brand and some deals are so logical that even a wannabe surfer can negotiate them!

To explore more about engaging celebrities to promote the brand, I sat down with *ZICO Coconut Water* founder (and my fellow weekend Stand Up Paddleboarder) Mark Rampolla and he provided the perfect example of another natural **Starfish** relationship that formed with surfing great Bethany Hamilton.

STARFISH

CASE STUDY

STARFISH SURFER GIRL

Mark Rampolla, founder of *ZICO Coconut Water* has always been interested in associating *ZICO* with the right **Starfish**. Like we have discussed, the company not only wants the celebrity to fit the brand perfectly: active, natural, healthy and authentic; but they must drink and really love *ZICO*. Mark and his team don't want stars that just hold up a *ZICO* package then drink some high-sugar, artificial garbage as soon as they walk away!

So when Mark's friend (who happened to be Bethany Hamilton's agent) introduced the two, imagine how happy he was when he showed up and she was drinking *ZICO*! Having grown up in Hawaii she always knew about and loved coconut water and when she discovered *ZICO* it become her beverage of choice. The agent thought it was a great fit, especially since she already loved *ZICO* so he approached the company's founder so they could meet.

Rampolla knew about Bethany and her amazing story. From a shark attack that took her arm as a youth to her current status as one of the world's top female surfers, she is an amazing inspiration and positive role model. The feature film *Soul Surfer* was based on her story and between her surfing awards, media appearances, and movie-star looks, she brings significant visibility and identifiability. Not only did Mark admire her, his wife and children were also fans of her incredible story, fearless yet humble nature and relaxed but competitive spirit and deep spirituality. She is such a great role model for so many people, kids and adults alike. And that combination of out-of-water character combined with her ability as a top competitor in the world of surfing, makes her a great **Starfish**.

Mark began by just making sure that she always had plenty of *ZICO*, even when she traveled around the world. When she spoke at the beverage's company event, she was very well received by the rest of the team and so they began to talk about her story on *ZICO's* website and Facebook page. Now that Bethany and *ZICO* have an established relationship that is as natural as the product itself, they are beginning to integrate her into retail and other promotions. It's an evolving, organic partnership built on mutual respect and common values and goals and Rampolla couldn't have asked for a more ideal representative to align with his brand!

Working with **Starfish** involves some of the most unusual variables that marketing minds can face. You could argue that the same passion for sports or entertainment or music that we engage fans with is a genuine factor in working with **Starfish**. I can't count how many times we were working on a sports brand where the spokesman had a big game, set a record or won the championship. You must always be prepared to go in one of several directions and that can be an exciting aspect of the job. You are working both ends with a "Congratulations" campaign ready to go if they win the championship and a Plan B communication strategy if they don't.

When the Arizona Cardinals were negotiating with Heisman Trophy winner Matt Leinart to be their new quarterback, we had several different ads ready to go at the flip of a switch. One was generic game tune-in for the network featuring the Cardinals. Another was geared towards Matt signing and actually making his debut. I believe we also had variations for him actually starting as well as him joining the team but not planning on playing. I remember scanning the news wire and waiting until the last minute to release the appropriate ad. Being topical and relevant with the **Starfish's** story integrates you into the conversation

Marketers understand that the value of a good spokesman can provide positive awareness. A high profile player can garner incremental value when they appear across various media. While a golfer like Phil Mickelson wears *Barclay's* or *Callaway* on his shirt, other endorsers rely on the relationship they have fostered with the celebrity to serve as their awareness. Kevin Hartman can't be holding a *ZICO* water while he plays (especially since those giant soccer goalie gloves wouldn't help) or have their logo on his jersey so the company incorporates an implied association. The marketers job is to build up a relationship between the **Starfish** and the brand so the consumer forms a Pavlovian response that triggers one with the other. Then, the extra exposure the sponsor gets second-hand when Hartman makes an amazing save and appears on *SportsCenter* hopefully sticks and drives a little incremental buzz for the brands he represents. A rising tide raises all ships so when an athlete does well, the brands reap the reward.

Which brings us to the unfortunate wipeout. As we've

seen with Tiger, Lance, and the other previous examples, **Starfish** can have a downside. (Don't those commercials of OJ Simpson running through the terminal for *Hertz* take on a whole new meaning now?) One of the other reasons I tend to incorporate retired players (aside from a much easier schedule and availability) is the fact that young, alpha-male athletes who have significant privilege and opportunity don't always make the best decisions. I'm speaking in general terms because there are incredibly responsible, loyal, and professional twenty-three year olds that would make great spokesmen. But current athletes who are young, single, and "bullet-proof" also tend to make more mistakes that could cause disgrace upon a brand or association.

As a more seasoned surfer, I have a voice in my head (I actually have a lot of voices in my head but that's for another day). When I'm getting ready to drop in on a big face and it looks a little steep and dangerous, the voice tells me I'm about to become sushi. While I don't *always* listen to it, I do tend to hear it more than I used to. The wear and tear on my body combined with experience and just plain mellowing has made me less likely to take risks so I'm less likely to embarrass myself... by drowning.

Younger people drive faster, party more, take risks, and

enjoy their current celebrity status. They say youth is wasted on the young and as a general rule of thumb, I find a former basketball great is more likely to stay out of trouble than a current NBA player. Just playing the odds.

Plus, the old pros are *pros*! They have done dozens of appearances, been exposed to all sorts of situations, and generally have the experience to exceed expectations. While everyone wants the hottest current celebrity to align with their brand, you can gain significant mileage out of the nostalgic route with a former great who appeals to the targeted demographic *and* their fathers! I often marvel at the patients and (either real or feigned) interest a Hall of Famer will demonstrate at an appearance when some hillbilly reminds the celeb that they once said hello at *Circle K* and the fan said, *"good game."* Twenty years later, the fan is at a signing asking if the player remembered that monumental interaction. Just once I would like to see my **Starfish** say, *"Yes! The three greatest moments of my life were winning the World Series, being there when my son was born, and giving you a high-five at the checkout line of the Piggly-Wiggly in 1994."*

When utilizing **Starfish**, it's important to maintain consistency. Don't bring on one type of celebrity and then go in the opposite approach unless it's specifically for the irony. Brands often struggle with a consistent message and if you don't know how to tell the story, how are your users supposed to know? Going the action sports route and having Shawn White as your pitchman is great but you can't then turn around and bring in a *Disney Channel* actor to attract girls. Just like in surfing, pick your line and stay the course. The **Starfish** is just like a logo or a tagline and needs to provide consistent, on-brand association.

Be sure when you are sourcing your next **Starfish** that you take into account that celebrity's overload factor. While certain icons can carry multiple brands, I often think it's important to "own" that celebrity so as not to incidentally promote another product. When Michael Jordan was in his prime, his face on TV could be representing *McDonalds, Gatorade, Nike, Upper Deck*... I tend to think the celebrity I'm bringing on should be my only date and not be involved with too many others. It's all about the bang for your buck and if you are splitting time, you are only getting half of the value.

Which brings us to ROI. Just like a digital banner or a print ad placement, we need to constantly monitor the **Starfish** value. Q scores are the measure to which the public feels the **Starfish** is believable and resonates. It measures effectiveness of a spokesman but not necessarily how they help *your* bottom line. Other companies like *BAT (Brand Affinity Technologies)* can help as well with their proprietary rating system. They rank the different variables like rate, fan awareness, etc to create a score that shows you the value for the talent you are securing.

I tend to monitor a control (generic ad), past campaigns, etc. against the **Starfish** version to ensure that the incremental blip exceeds the cost of the relationship. Just like the direct mail model where you measure A against B, you can overlay the celeb's version against a standard ad to determine the incremental value. While there is a "wow" factor to doing celebrity-based campaigns, it still boils down to a marketing tactic that has accountability. Because at the end of the day, a **Starfish** that costs you money without significant ROI is not the player you want on your roster.

STARFISH

SURF LESSON

A Starfish is born

Assuming you have found the right

ambassador for your company, let's look at ways to leverage them. In this SURF LESSON we will outline a few tactics and some do's and don'ts to help you activate the relationship and maximize your *Starfish*.

1) Packaging- If you plan on using your celebrity on pack, you should first determine the usage rights and strategy (i.e. uniform, league rules, etc.) While your creative director may coordinate a photo shoot with the celebrity, be sure you have a direction versus generic "glory shots". Within the campaign theme, be sure you list all of the obvious as well as *possible* uses. If the *Starfish* is interacting with the product, make sure the star of the show isn't just the athlete instead of the brand. The glamor shot of a candy bar looks enticing standing alone with an industry food modeling pro making it look delicious under perfect lighting. The same candy looks puny and not worth the money if some big

6'8" power forward with huge mitts makes it look like a teeny bite-sized treat.

2) On-air - The crowned jewel in an athlete's portfolio is appearing in a TV commercial. But just because you have the player, it might not be the right move. Some *Starfish* are pros in front of the camera and you may have hired the actor or singer because they absolutely glow on the screen.   I have also worked with athletes who tend to make it a little difficult because they have taken one too many to the head or just don't have the on-air touch.

Remember that the personality, attractiveness, and likability are as important as on-field stats. When writing or reviewing a script, ensure the *Starfish* has several versions of the lines and that it reads naturally. If they have to use technical terms or scientific jargon, it won't appear genuine.

Also, with digital content being a key to multi-platform activations, get plenty of behind-the-scene shots, testimonials, interviews, bloopers, etc. You can always pass on footage but you can't go back in time and create missed shots.

I often check with the Sales department or similar distribution points to see if there is any special shout-outs or personalized videos the *Starfish* can do. Customized clips where the celebrity gives a personal message to the retail decision maker or grocery buyer goes a long way. Create a list of your top VIPs so you can have the *Starfish* do a little blurb.

3) Events - Let's outline the purpose of the event and then the different types of activations that support the effort. Make a list of the goals of your event:

A) Drive awareness for your brand.

B) Drive traffic for your retail location or retail partner who distributes your product.

C) Associate your brand with the **Starfish** in the eyes of consumers.

D) Garner press/media and buzz using the **Starfish** as the focus of the story.

4) Once you've determined the objective, you can begin to plan out the details to ensure you get the most bang for your buck. Cover all of your bases in order to maximize your relationship with the celebrity. You want to ensure everything at the event screams your brand and the partnership with your selected **Starfish**.

To bring in traffic for a consumer event, we utilize local players that resonate in that town and are less expensive than the national all-time legends. A player has significantly more appeal in their own market of course (as we discussed in the previous Scottsbluff CASE STUDY) and locals will flock to a lesser known star that played for their local team.

Make sure you have plenty of signage and the local media comes out to get an interview with the local star. For those who take pictures of (or if the *Starfish* is willing... *with*) the celebrity, make sure the talent is positioned in front of your logo so all social media posts or forwards include your brand.

As we discussed with the *Remora*, a radio remote is a great partner-ship especially with talent. You give them content and they give you exposure. Same with the local paper and television stations. Your media checklist for events should include all the local (and some-times national) press. And even if they don't want to send a reporter out, you can usually get in the weekend *Events* section for a little more weight in the impressions.

While I am better with celebrity talent than I am with surfing, I wanted to provide some insight from one of the industry's all-time big wave gurus when it comes to endorsements... Super Agent Leigh Steinberg. I sat with Leigh and discussed his philosophies, experience, and cases for this book and many of his theories and proven tactics align with my experience. Leigh is a pioneer in the athlete representation world dating back to the 70's when he represented a young QB named Steve Bartkowski and has since worked with some of the greatest names in sports and entertainment including Steve Young, Oscar de la Hoya, Troy Aikman, Howie Long, and more.

When discussing how a brand or product needs to be organic to the **Starfish**, we talked about how smart marketing professionals think. They analyze all of the factors and variables we previously discussed and then need to apply an organic campaign that is both believable as well as memorable.

It's not enough with today's high-stakes contracts to throw away money on a **Starfish** that doesn't move your brand. Along with the actor or athlete's story, the marketing people need to craft a tale that attracts casual fans as well as the die-hards. Leigh discussed a fun commercial he did for a phone company with Hall of Fame Quarterback Warren Moon (the same great athlete who once made fun of me for my surfboard fin in the rear-end story). In the spot, it focused on how close the agent and the player were and how frequently they spoke with one another... on the company's phone. It was organic, direct, and made sense to the viewer. That's a win-win as it allowed for a peak into the lives of a Super Agent and his client while demonstrating how **Starfish** use the product in their everyday lives.

It was well crafted, on-target and moving. But unlike the phone example where everything was planned out and expected, sometimes a large set of waves will jump up out of nowhere and give you the unexpected ride of your life. The unpredictability of sports that makes Jeremy Lin go from D-League to "LinSanity" superstar overnight is a powerful entity. That's the sports/celebrity variable that makes this marketing element so fluid and if you can adjust your surfing style on the fly, you can capitalize on an unforeseen marketing opportunity!

STARFISH

CASE STUDY

A CLOSE SHAVE

In 2006, Leigh Steinberg was the agent representing Pittsburgh Steelers' QB Ben Roethlisberger. Big Ben was a little superstitious as athletes tend to be and when the team won a big game that season in which the QB hadn't shaved, Ben decided not to shave until they lost.

Before long, the Steelers are making their Super Bowl run and Ben is looking like an MVP and a lumberjack all in one. His unkempt facial hair is growing almost as fast as the buzz and media attention around him. And ever the opportunist, Leigh wanted to capitalize on the situation and Big Ben's big beard.

Working with the agency representing *Gillette* razors, Leigh brokered a deal with the company. The plan was that Ben would shave off his beard using their product. All he needed to do was win the Super Bowl and the deal was done.

After some back-and-forth negotiations, Leigh had put together a plan to not only have Ben serve as a **Starfish** to endorse the company, but the QB would also have his now infamous facial hair shaved off utilizing a *Gillette* product at the company's post-game press conference. Once the Steelers beat the Seahawks 21-10 (by more than a hair) it was time for Big Ben to become clean shaven, "Bald" Ben.

As most of you can imagine, winning a Super Bowl brings on significant time commitments for the stars of the game. Along with team celebrations, family, media obligations, etc., the players are pushed and pulled in many directions (although since that means they won the game, they don't complain). When timing didn't look good for Roethlisberger to make the *Gillette* press conference, it was up to Steinberg to create a solution. Knowing Ben was to appear on *The Late Show with David Letterman*, the agent offered up a can't-miss opportunity for the new partner... having Letterman shave off Ben's beard on live TV!

After a little coordination, the plan went off without a hitch. The media and national attention the beard shaving stunt garnered was significantly more than the athlete or the agency had originally anticipated and it made the partnership incrementally more successful. Along with the buzz the Super Bowl winning QB garners even if it was a straight product endorsement, the tie-in with the beard, the unusual story of Letterman shaving him, and the more-than-logical use of a fine *Gillette* product to accomplish the task all made for an amazing campaign that surely had the agency and marketing folks at *Gillette* feeling as sharp as their blades (or as sharp as Big Ben looked afterwards.)

"There are no more committed people on the planet than surfers. We fall down a lot. We turn around, paddle back out, and do it over and over again. Unlike anything else in life, the stoke of surfing is so high that the failures quickly fade from memory."

- Gary Sirota

CHAPTER 11

SHARKS

If competition is viewed as **Sharks**, and the largest major competitors are the apex killer, the great white shark, then we have an instant picture of the competitive nature of practically every marketing category. The coral reef is a perfect analogy to use for describing our business environment as there are literally millions of friends and foes circling around you at all times.

Sharks are the obvious foe because they are aggressive and would be on your groups' radar as the #1 competition in your space. *Pepsi* vs. *Coke*, *ABC* vs. *NBC*, or *Ford* vs. *Toyota*. These feared predators will attack anyone in their way and will either consciously or indirectly based on their presence; affect many smaller brands trying to survive. The bulls and tiger **Sharks** are the companies that tend to do the side-by-side comparison and spend as much money attacking the competition as they do building up their own brand. They were doing *Super PAC* slander ads way before the 2012 election made it commonplace. The *Apple* spots with the young cool guy vs. the nerdy PC, the countless taste tests between soda companies, and pretty much every political campaign on-air feature a splashing mess of teeth, blood, and guts. If you find yourself in a feeding frenzy with these jaw-chomping competitors, get ready for some damage because even the largest great whites have significant scarring on their bodies from other sharks' teeth. You may survive the war but is it worth the collateral damage?

But like your competition, **Sharks** come in all shapes and sizes. Don't assume they are all meat-eating killers because while the bull, tiger, and great white will strike fear in a surfer's heart, there are leopards, horned sharks, and nurses who won't harm you or your brand unless you are a smaller little morsel. They too will try to survive and go about their business but in a less aggressive way and only attack if you are direct competition as they prefer a symbiotic lifestyle. You need not worry about a similar sized brand selling potato chips if you are marketing travel services. Aside from general traffic and overexposure of messages across the board, we don't concern ourselves with being attacked by a non-category competitor. Just as competition isn't always predictable and you should monitor the rivals on a routine basis, plan and execute your strategy accordingly and keep in mind that it's not always as dangerous as you may think. After all, the biggest shark in the world, the whale shark, eats plankton and is harmless to surfers.

The more aggressive **Sharks** however may be out to make a meal of you and we need to look beyond just the big rows of teeth in front of you and realize there are many different forms of competition that will nibble away at you and your business as well. Sometimes its the smaller nips on the dorsal fin that slowly erode your market share, not the gaping mouth in front of you.

Competition from a smaller, less threatening species like a **Crab** doesn't directly take your business instantly. Their cost-effective approach runs at such a low overhead by utilizing previously built factories (shells), existing channels of distribution, etc. that they can run lean and mean and be living in *your* shell before you know it! The market share they take is minimal on the surface but over time, they can start to grow enough to get on your radar. These **Crabs** steal a little share every day and as they grow and get stronger, you often find little nips being taken from your bottom line until you start to feel an aggregate of the blows.

The start-up beer brewed in the garage may be insignificant to *Coors* but after dozens of local and regional efforts, they may be gaining momentum and now looking to steal a little shelf space. (See the *Cruz Del Sol Tequila* CASE STUDY later in this chapter for an actual sample of this dynamic in action). Now they are no longer a bystander if they are getting more and more of your domain and poking their ugly little **Crab** antenna out of their shell more.

Then there are the crafty competitor like the master of mimic; the **Octopus**. These brands are always a half step behind the innovator and quick to make their brand as similar to the leading product as possible. It's not creative but it is safe. Like a school of fish, they would like to create as many similarities as possible to ensure they are at least in the consumer's vision without having to do all of the work building a category. The main culprit in the world of imitation, **Octopi** have a survival strategy to change their appearance to blend in. There's a reason why less expensive brands or "house brands" utilize the same color patterns and style of the more successful, and pricier, name brands. It's like an octopus camouflaging to look like his surroundings. While it's a proven survival strategy and a cost-effective way to exist in the market, there isn't much to discuss other than to see what the category leaders do and camouflage yourself to look as similarly as you can. It's a decent (albeit not very sexy) way to gain share by imitating the category leader and mimicking your name/product as closely and as similarly as possible to attract consumers.

I take particular offense at these late adaptor, trend-following eight-leggers! The companies that are content with zero innovation, no R&D, and no original thought goes against my entire platform of creative marketing. But you have to at least accept that their is a niche in the **Tide Pool** that these companies can flourish in and as long as they are content producing boring, me-too efforts, they can do well. When they build the second tablet to compete with the *iPad* or the private label bread that is $1.00 less per loaf, they need to be tracked and monitored just like the big **Shark** who you watch constantly. Otherwise you might not see this "threat" cutting into your revenue.

I'm fairly certain that given ideal conditions, any surfer would love to have the break all to himself. Any fish would love to own the rocks. And any marketer would love to eliminate competition. But just as in nature, business tends to be a crowded lagoon. People often focus so much on their own efforts and branding that they fail to see the large dorsal fin circling. It's the **Shark's** nature to hunt and it is the marketer's responsibility to know and understand the competitive landscape. Whether it's fight, flight, or choose to coexist, as long as you account for the competition, you have covered a key element to success. And always remember once a large predator enters the scene; you don't need to be able to out-swim a **Shark**, just be able to out-swim the surfers you are with.

SHARKS

SURF LESSON

CHECK FOR FINS

In warmer locations like Florida and Hawaii, most tourists don't know that they are being watched by the most feared animal in the world. Sharks are found all over the tropical waters and if you stop and look, you'd be amassed at how many predators are lurking nearby.

Let's look at who your **Sharks** (competition) are and how we can align the different strategies within the book you can utilize to compete. To explore your competitors and understand the other fish swimming in your space, simply list the following:

A) My direct competitor(s) who has the same product or service is/are:

B) In terms of a direct threat to take business from me, I would rank them in the following order (starting with the biggest threat as a "1" and going on from there.) I would qualify them as A) **Shark** B) **Octopus** C) **Crab**

C) What do they do better than us? What do we do better than them?

D) If they were able to get the tidal report and could beat us to the best surf break based on one main advantage, what would it be? And how would we combat that strike? If some **Sharks** are just bigger and stronger, then what assets do we have to enable us to camouflage, swim away, or pick off customers?

E) Take everything they do well, all of the resources or advantages we have, and write up your plan of attack. Remember, you can fight off a **Shark** if you have the proper technique. A good punch in the nose will turn away even the largest attacker and you simply need to have a plan that allows you to properly know when, where, and how hard to punch.

For those of you analytical types who I probably insulted previously by dubbing you "spreadsheet marketers" you can always do a *Competitive Array* assessment to enable a quantifiable score. Much like a surfing competition, even though the spirit of the sport is to push yourself and create your own style and experience, there are scoring mechanisms that can allow you to quantify your competition beyond the previous **Sharks** SURF LESSON. It provides a quantitative scoring system to allow you to best assign numeric rankings to your competitive landscape.

To create your own *Competitive Array* to determine the actual importance or threat of the **Sharks** in your space, try the following SCORECARD SURF LESSON:

SHARKS

SURF LESSON

SCORECARD

In trying to identify your competition and see what types of **Sharks** are out there, try creating a *Competitive Array.* To best assign a score to each of the competitors you will be up against, try doing the following:

A) Define exactly what your industry consists of - What is the scope and nature of the business? Create a matrix that we can fill in and create a chart for.

B) Determine who your competitors are. List the direct competition across the top of the matrix allowing columns for both rating and their weighted score. And don't forget those little **Sharks** that might not be a huge threat but still affect your bottom line.

C) Determine who your customers are and what benefits you will provide them. What exactly are their expectations with your goods/ services?

D) Establish the key factors or benchmarks for success in your industry.

E) Next, rate and assign a ranking for these key success factors by giving each one a weighting score of less than one. Assuming that the entire sum of all the weightings must add up to one, apply a number to each individual score that appears as a decimal.

F) After you've applied a score to the success benchmark, rate each of your *Sharks* on each of the key success factors on a scale of one to ten.

G) Now that you have the successes and *Sharks* assigned a numerical value, multiply each cell in the matrix by the factor weighting. You might be surprised that your perceived biggest foe scores a 3.9 while the secondary **Shark** that you were not as concerned with scored a 6.3!

Sharks come in all shapes and sizes as we know and they are not all the blood-thirsty enemies we envision. Some are smaller animals that eat tiny crabs and are not always swimming around looking to bite you in half. Knowing what types of competitors (AKA predators) are in your surfing area is wise. Understanding the interest, aggressiveness, and temperament of your competition will allow you to best navigate the environment.

There are several different ways to determine who might be a **Shark** for your business and while the ways to uncover and identify who your competition is might be infinite, the more research and understanding you have, the better your business model will be.

For the sake of marketing, we would focus on the *Four P's* and ensure that we spend our time outlining the market share, growth, demographics, promotional mix, channels of distribution, costs/pricing, etc. Most of the basics you've been exposed to by this point so we need not tell a surfer that "this is a board" and "there is the ocean".

But there are contemporary resources that provide up-to-the-minute insight into the **Sharks** in your waters: digital and social media platforms. I spoke with a very senior executive and he told me he didn't like the idea of engaging the enemy's Facebook and Twitter feeds because in his opinion, he was adding size to their followers and supporting what they do. I informed him that, much like sticking a tracking device on a great white, it allows you to directly monitor their communication and business. Seeing when they promote their products, what pricing or specials they announce, and what their consumers like/dislike is priceless intel! And going back to the CASE STUDY *(Go F- Yourself!)* in the previous chapter, you can see what resonates with your demographic and avoid the same fate as ill-advised surfers who drop in on the wrong waves.

One thing that tends to be overlooked when dealing with **Sharks** is the emotional element. People say "it's just business" but yet it still brings forth emotions and feelings that can affect your decision making. They mom-and-pop store that has a huge supermarket go in next door is going to be significantly more emotional about the new arrangement than the district manager for the grocery chain. It's human nature. And the *fear* of a shark attack is significantly more prevalent than the actual risk of attack.

The various decisions marketers make, which is ironically to evoke passion and drive responses from emotional consumers, should try to be made with a clear head. Eliminating emotion from the marketing mix will help create stronger strategic direction and ultimately better results. The elements of the campaign to combat or thwart the competition should drive emotion, but not be established based on it.

If you are surfing your local break and large, grey shadow glides underneath you, it's hard to say not to get your heart racing. Any surfer can tell you that the overwhelming majority of things that are sharing your beach come with the territory and the mental image of what that large shadow was is probably worse than what it really is.

Take it from a guy who once had a brush against my leg by a large creature. After my initial jump-out-of-the-water like Scooby Doo (running in midair), I was soon comforted by a dozen fellow surfers who were amused and laughing at the seal behind me. (Although some say it was the octave of the girlish screech that came from my pie hole!) Again, analyze the **Sharks** in your water with your head and not your heart!

We are all **Sharks** in some sense. Every one of us in business is in competition with someone somewhere. While we see the competition as **Sharks** (or a **Crab** or an **Octopus**) remember that they also see *you* as competition. It never hurts to engage a little self-awareness and determine how you appear to your competitors and to what level of a threat you might be. Sometimes, just plugging along and keeping your head down as a **Crab** can attract unwanted attention and lure in larger predators. If you have a business-generating niche or have started to gain some traction in your field, rest assured you will have company soon. Like a surfer splashing in the water, you *will* attract attention.

SHARKS

CASE STUDY

CRUZ ALONG

There are lots of competitive industries in the world and one of the most cut-throat is the wine, beer, and spirits business. From retail and grocery chains to the bars and restaurants, this multi-billion dollar industry is not just dominated by **Sharks**, but more like schools of great whites!

Cruz del Sol Tequila (AKA *Cruz Tequila*) is a high-end craft spirit that was originally launched in Arizona by a team of passionate connoisseurs looking to make the world's most outstanding tequila. Lead by its entrepreneurial owners, the brand quickly grew into a critically acclaimed spirit and the darling of boutique beverages.

There are several tools that the booze biz relies on for marketing including more than its fair share of tastings, booth babes, and bar night promotions. *Cruz Tequila*, looking to establish itself as an "ultra premium" high end alternative to the well marketed corporate brands, held true to its promise of better quality and a better experience than the much larger **Sharks** that had dominated the category. *Cruz Tequila* relied on tastings to showcase their product, earned accolades in trade publications, and stuck to a higher brand quality than "free shot" nights. And supported by an amazing product within the shimmery triangular blown-glass bottle, the marketing strategy worked. Too well.

Before long, *Cruz Tequila* was the tequila of choice in many Phoenix hot spots (and having attended ASU myself, I can say that *those* folks know their booze!) Without sacrificing their image and quality, *Cruz Tequila* maintained their high-end stance and drove their own revenue while increasing sales for the locations they were being poured at. The company could be characterized as a **Crab** to their competitors because they plugged along and slowly absorbed more and more of the market share without making a huge, single splash. Larger brands that had dominated the same locations were now being put to the side in favor of a better product.

As we know about **Sharks**, they don't like to go without eating! So well-funded tequila companies approached the business the only way they knew how; throw around enough muscle so that the *little-tequila-that-could* would eventually be forced out. The competition started undercutting the price of their own products, doing two-for-one nights, bringing in the models with free premiums, and basically throwing their money and weight around to drown *Cruz Tequila* out.

When word got out that the larger, cheap tequila was basically being given away, the crowds started to flock to the bar that *Cruz Tequila* once dominated. Classic success of the larger great white over the smaller guy, right? Wrong.

The bar, once a vibrant, upscale restaurant that serviced a loyal, consistent clientele suddenly started to attract "the wrong element" looking to make every night Spring Break. These were non-discriminating consumers who valued cheap, heavily marketed booze brands, but whose loyalties were fleeting.

Soon the average cost per tab dropped dramatically, the bar's normal customers felt pushed out, *Cruz Tequila*'s sales fell off as the brand was successful in giving away their product to reclaim market share.   The successful eatery became a "dive bar" and fueled by the large **Sharks** giving away cheap tequila, and fights became the standard.

Before long, the bar wasn't making money, the staff was constantly breaking up fights and policing a lower-level consumer, and having more issues than they ever bargained for. The big tequila company basically succeeded in driving the bar under in an effort to attack a smaller, popular competitor. The self-destructive plan did indeed accomplish their goal of slowing *Cruz Tequila*... but at a cost of losing significant money in the process and eventually hurting themselves with a lost client when the bar was forced to go under. Sometimes the competition is a blood- thirsty predator too blind to see that they are taking everyone down with them.

The bar has indeed learned their lesson and when they reopened, once again positioned as an upscale eatery, their relationship with *Cruz Tequila* did not disappear as their sales did, and *Cruz*

Tequila continues to be poured for the discerning consumer and win gold medals at festival after festival. So all we can do is have a toast to the ignorant **Shark** that would rather bring others down instead of drive their brand up.

Salud, *Cruz del Sol*!

"It's not tragic to die doing something you love"

- Mark Foo

CONCLUSION (SUNSET)

The sun slowly drops upon the horizon and another incredible day of surfing (and marketing) comes to a close. Not every wave was perfect. Not every ride was epic. But you surfed and that makes it a better day than when you woke up.

You worked to create and promote a brand, company or initiative and communicated the value of what you are doing. You were able to apply your experience, strategy, creativity, passion, and effort to advance the cause. You are a marketer and by association, a surfer.

To review some of the general principles and philosophies in *The Surfers Guide To Marketing* we start with finding our inner-surfer. Not the stereotypical *"gnarly dude!"* character but more of the Zen-like, passionate, soul surfer. The surfer who lives for the best waves, best conditions, adapts their style to what's on the horizon, and the appreciation of everything leading up to it. Similar to marketers, they constantly think about their art, how they can partake in their chosen activity and what tools they have at their disposal to create the ideal conditions. In that regard, marketers are surfers on dry land.

Even if your company is a huge Top 10 brand, you probably still don't have the budget, resources, or green light to do everything you'd like to with your product or service. We can all spend money, but as most of us don't have an unlimited checkbook, we need to find ways to maximize our resources. Utilizing the **Puffer Fish**, **Barnacle**, **Trojan (Sea) Horse** or **Starfish** techniques might provide you with opportunities to compete. Facing off against larger **Sharks**, combating the copycat **Octopus**, or even battling your brand's own limitations are challenges that you will need to address.

Leveraging the assets or creativity available to you and targeting the **Tide Pool** that best suites you, will allow you to slide down the face, get inside a barrel, and have an amazing ride or promotional campaign.

It's not about what you have, but rather what you do. The examples and CASE STUDIES of what smart marketers from surfers to Super Agents created for everything from tacos to tequila with sometimes (literally) no money. From stand-alone efforts to associating with partners at the world's largest events, hopefully the real-world examples highlighted in the book will serve as a blueprint or even as motivational model to show you that anything is possible.

Like surfers, marketers are extreme optimists and the only thing that will stop you is... you. Sure dropping in on a 12-foot face might cause you to quickly think about your plan (and your next of kin) but as they say, *"no guts, no glory."* You may not pull off every wave and have an *Endless Summer* afternoon but if you position yourself well, push the limits, and never stop paddling, I'm confident you will end up with a huge day of surfing and a portfolio of successful campaigns.

My promise to you, the reader/marketer/surfer, was that I would communicate, motivate, and entertain and I am (as a disciple of my own teachings) optimistically satisfied that I accomplished all three. We discussed traditional and unique marketing efforts, utilized actual cases and proven examples of the techniques, and created working SURF LESSONS to help you apply the concepts, provided anecdotes that put marketing efforts in actual context or illustrated by using surfing vernacular. Through it all, committed to the basic philosophy that surfing and marketing both provide satisfaction and fulfillment if you simple believe that every wave is a new opportunity for an epic ride, I am confident I am proof that every surfer has their day, every marketer has an opportunity, and every sunset allows both to reflect on a job well done.

Mahalo!

ABOUT THE AUTHOR

Randy Rovegno has over two decades of successful marketing experience working on brands including *ESPN, ABC, FOX, AT&T, NFL, Upper Deck*, and more. As an avid surfer and former amateur stand-up comedian (who stinks at both), Rovegno speaks to various university classes about marketing strategy, real-world case studies, and navigating today's marketing landscape utilizing his unique portfolio, experience, and humor to motivate tomorrow's marketing minds.

After stints in various CPG and consumer marketing groups and in a key role with a boutique agency that he quickly developed into a multi-million dollar business, he founded LONGBOARD Marketing in 2008 because nothing spells success like a start-up in the worst economy in 20 years.

As a creative executive challenged with developing novel and successful campaigns for the most dynamic, savvy sports and entertainment clients in the world, Rovegno must constantly utilize creativity and unorthodox tactics to drive the products or brands he works with. It is based on the various challenges and successes from his award-winning career that motivated him to write this book and demonstrate some of the favorite tricks of the trade.

It's ironic that the author who makes at least 500 surfing references might just be the worst surfer in the ocean. With a surfing resume that includes multiple trips to the ER, more time held under the waves than kelp, and a style that has earned him the nickname the *"Yeti from the Jetty"* it is a foregone conclusion that what he lacks in surfing ability, he makes up for in proven marketing success.

The married father of two is very proud to bring his marketing experience to life and now he can check "author" off of his bucket list. And the way he surfs, that list just might expire before you finish reading this page.

www.ingramcontent.com/pod-product-compliance
Lightning Source LLC
Chambersburg PA
CBHW071402170526
45165CB00001B/149